CAMALDOLI

A Journey into its History & Spirituality

———

Lino Vigilucci OSB CAM.

Translated by

Peter–Damian Belisle OSB CAM.

SOURCE BOOKS

HERMITAGE BOOKS

CALIFORNIA

Text copyright © Edizioni Camaldoli, 1988
English Translation © Peter-Damian Belisle OSB CAM., 1995

Originally Published by Edizioni Camaldoli, Monastero di Camaldoli
(AR) Italia, 1988
First English Edition 1995

Library of Congress Cataloging-in-Publication Data
Vigilucci, Lino.
[Camaldoli. English]
Camaldoli : a journey into its history & spirituality / Lino Vigilucci
: translated by Peter–Damian Belisle.
p.   cm.
Includes bibliographical references
ISBN 0-940147-37-8
1. Camaldolese--History. 2. Romuald, Saint. ca. 951-1027
3. Camaldolese--Biography. 4. Christian saints--Italy--Biography.
5. Camaldolese--Spiritual life. I. Title.
BX3085.V5413   1995
271'.14--dc20   95–14280
CIP

ISBN: 0-940147-37-8

A Publication of Source Books and Hermitage Books

    P.O. Box 794
    Trabuco Canyon
    CA 92678
    U.S.A.

Printed by KNI Inc., Anaheim, CA.

Dedication & Acknowledgments

A warm and profound thanks to my confrere
Ugo Fossa for his generous and competent
contribution. —*Lino Vigilucci osb cam.*

•

I wish to thank Br. Ezekiel Lotz, Camaldolese, for his
generous assistance in proofreading the
translation manuscript.

And I would like to dedicate the work of this translation
to our present and future novices who come to embrace the
amazing story of Camaldoli. —*Peter–Damian Belisle osb cam.*

Contents

Introductory Remarks

These pages will not say much to the scholars and critics, but they will say something to those who come to Camaldoli for the first time, or often, and who come out of spiritual need.

Situated almost at the center of the Tuscan-Romagnese Apennine mountain chain, including the Alps of Saint Benedict and the Serra Alps descending from Falterona (1654 m.) towards Spillo (1459 m.) as far as the Mandrioli Pass (1173 m.), this area holds a charm and particular appeal which distinguishes it from the many interesting areas of the upper and lower Casentino region.

Camaldoli's history begins in the eleventh century when Saint Romuald—abbot, hermit and courageous reformer—arrived there and began the foundation of the Hermitage and the Monastery which lies below. With his Papal Bull dated November 4, 1113, Pope Paschal II gave the monks a considerable boost by annexing to Camaldoli some hermitages and monasteries already founded or reformed by Saint Romuald, thereby enabling the source for a cenobitical-eremitical Congregation headed by Camaldoli and called, for that reason 'Camaldolese.'

The ensuing centuries certainly had their times of alternating prosperity and deterioration, but that particular nature of Camaldoli has been preserved for our own time, expressing today a specific and unique mark within the context of the whole western monasticism in its marriage of Hermitage and Monastery.

Unlike nearly all the Romualdian foundations which fell victim to the wear-and-tear of time, and sooner or later vanished, Camaldoli continued to exist faithful to the founder's design. For contemporary humanity it continues as it has been in the past: a citadel of the Spirit; a living cell in the tissue of the Church; a vital space in the spiritual and historical structure of Benedictine monasticism and Christian harmony.

The main aim of the merely informative character of these pages is to offer, as if through a series of snapshots, a first point of contact with the history and spiritual message of this monastic core in its various articulations. Identified almost immediately with Camaldoli, the role of 'head and mother' of a congregation with the same name forces us to enlarge the aperture so the reader can come to recognize other places and persons outside Camaldoli, but surely trained in the school of its tradition. This allows us to point out specific, essential elements which are foundational to that pluralism which we call, quite simply, 'Camaldolese' and which always presents itself as the most characteristic mark of this institution.

I have deliberately refrained from any critical notes on controversial historical questions, nor have I commented on the behavior of some through whose influence any part of the genuine face of primitive Camaldolese unity was altered. Still, the quoted information is all well-documented and comparable, so I do not presume to present anything in arbitrary or simply approximate fashion.

The figure of Saint Romuald the founder, is treated at some length: with emphasis on his personal aspects more than on the merely statistical. The entire history and very style of Camaldolese life could not be grasped without an adequate knowledge of Romuald's rich personality, as well as of his influence as reformer and 'spiritual director.' Convinced of this, after an indispensible outline of Camaldoli's origin and the formation of a congregation of the same name, I have tried to furnish a sort of gallery of some of the more significant disciples and followers in whom we can discern the touch or signature of the master: Romuald's fatherhood.

Camaldoli is now on the threshold of a millenium of history. The monks who live there today pray God that such a long journey continue as a living presence, not just an archeological fact.

Lino Vigilucci 1988

Here is Macarius, here is Romuald,
here are my brothers who halted their feet
inside the cloister and kept their hearts firm.

DANTE, IL PARADISO, CAN.22,49-51

LORENZO MONACO: SAINT ROMUALD (952 C.– 1027)
MINIATURE FROM CORALE 8 C.76 1395 LAURENZIANA (FL)

one:

The Founder

1. Journey of a man

The interest in Camaldoli and its development has been associated decisively with the name and brilliant creation of one man: Saint Romuald, abbot (+1027). Before he arrived there, this Apennine tract of central Italy surely had its own local name, but the industrious and intelligent eleventh-century reformer, professional monk and hermit, would make it famous. The history of Camaldoli begins with the history of Romuald; the two are identified with one another so much that, though there are two names, there is really but one event. Familiarity with one leads to familiarity with the other.

We do not know the day of Saint Romuald's birth and the year is debatable. But we do know his ethnic, familial and socio-religious origins. He was born at Ravenna around the middle of the tenth century when Roman-Byzantine Ravenna was so endearing to Emperor Otto the Great that he wanted to build there a great palace for himself and his court. The Church of Ravenna was then tended by Peter, archbishop and feudal lord responsible for the pastoral care of Christ's flock and the safekeeping of the imperial holdings. Romuald's father was Duke Sergio, a Lombard descendant of strong character, authoritarian, and skillful at wielding the sword. We do not know the name of Romuald's mother, nor whether he had brothers or sisters.

These personal data—his native lineage, Lombard origin, and noble family name, a lifetime spanning the tenth and eleventh (the 'iron') centuries—form a background for the life and to a certain extent, the personality of this man whose

1

character was quite different from his father's. Romuald was gentle, opposed to class quarrels, reflective by nature, and not in the least avaricious. His childhood is cloaked in the silence of the sources, except for one annotation of Saint Peter Damian [1]† who tells us that, although our saint was from a moneyed family, he was not given any literary instruction.[2] As far as his adolescence is concerned, Peter Damian hints at temptations which the young duke suffered in the flesh.[3] His youth reveals something which points toward the future of this lively young man. He often roamed the pine woods of Ravenna in search of game and at the same time engrossed in God, stopping as if to relish the deep silence and whisper: "How well could hermits remain here in the depths of these woods; with what peace could they live, far from the world's clamor!" [4] And while there was a rapid succession of desires and future projects coursing through his mind, it was as though he could foresee what heaven was preparing for him.[5]

One day Romuald's father told him that there would be no hunting. He wanted his son to accompany him outside the city to settle an old argument with his cousin who claimed rights to territory which did not belong to him. Opposed to such disputes by temperament, the young man had to obey his father, against his own will. Arguments over the land had continued for some time but every attempt at accommodation proved fruitless. To settle the matter, the Duke and his cousin decided to fight a duel and Romuald was forced to serve as his father's second.

Sergio won the duel and haughtily felt vindicated, even content in his heart. But Romuald was horrified at the sight of his father spilling blood. Added to the horror was the remorse he felt at being forced against his will to assist in the crime. The ecclesiastical canons of the day demanded a penance of forty days for such offences. The young son of the Duke decided on the spot to go and knock at the monastery gate of Saint Apollinare in Classe. He went there not so much to seek God, but in order to expiate the ugly,

---

† Textual notes and references are compiled at the end of the book.

bloody business in which he himself had only passively participated. He would spend forty days in the cloister. But once inside, he found the affair had left him desolate to the point that he would not leave. In fact, he asked for the monastic habit. But we will have Peter Damian tell the story:

'One day, while he was intensely praying to God, his mind was enkindled unexpectedly with such a great fire of divine love by the Holy Spirit that he suddenly burst into tears... He prostrated himself at the monks' feet and requested with indescribable longing to be clothed in the monastic habit. But the monks did not feel they could risk opening the door to his conversion because they were afraid of his father's severity. Onesto, who had once been the abbot of the cenobium of Classe, was then occupying Ravenna's archiepiscopal throne. Romuald went to him immediately and shared with him all of his heart's desire. The archbishop quite happily added his own incentive, encouraging Romuald's chaste desire, and ordered the brethren to receive him at once into their community. Protected by the archbishop's approval, the cenobites safely welcomed Romuald and gave him the habit of holy religion.'[6]

The outburst which accompanied the beginnings of Romuald's monastic journey quickly began to diminish as he recognized the great disparity between what the Rule demanded and how those monks were actually living. He began to experience conflict between his surroundings and the sincerity of his ardor. His first reaction was to flee. Monastic life at Saint Apollinare in Classe appeared extremely disappointing. In any case, it was lived contemptibly. The novice ventured his observations when necessary, 'quoting the precepts of the Rule, much to their consternation.'[7] A hatred welled up within the monks, suggesting to them that they should get rid of Romuald by killing him. They planned the crime but could not execute it because Romuald had been warned by one of the conspirators. Now he understood that he need persevere no longer, and the idea of leaving the monastery of Classe right away took clearer shape in his mind. He had heard that a certain hermit named Marino lived near Venice. Going to him seemed the best solution. His abbot and the monks not only gave him 'permission in the end,'[8] but even sighed with relief. Good zeal and sincerity always discriminate between good servants and the wicked. So after three years of suffering he left, but with the fruits of experience which would be most precious to him later on. Little did he realize that this departure from Classe would be a key moment in his life.

Marino was one of those hermits who lived in complete solitude, throughout Italy around the tenth century. We do not know exactly where Romuald would have found Marino's hermitage. Peter Damian simply says that it was 'in the area of Venice.'[9] We know more about Marino's gifts and the general tenor of his life. Peter Damian describes him as 'a man of simple soul, of great austerity and purity. He had come to the hermitage without any instruction on the doctrine of the eremitical life, and was driven there only by the impulse of good will. Throughout the year he would eat only half a slice of bread and a handful of beans on three days of the week. The other three days he added a little wine and something cooked.'[10] He prayed often. The Psalter was his norm and guide. Such was the spiritual master to whom Romuald now presented himself.

He brought with him the bloom of youth, a sincere love for seeking God, and the experience of those three years at Classe which had already marked his soul. But Romuald had undergone no instruction; he even had trouble reading. Master Marino, rather coarse and wild, was in favor of quick methods. 'Romuald, who had come illiterate from the world, opened the Psalter and barely managed to get through the words of the verses he touched. Moreover, keeping his eyes fixed on the book caused him fatigue and intolerable boredom. With all that, Marino struck the left side of Romuald's thick head with a rod he was holding in his hand, and Romuald sat down across from him. After much suffering, Romuald felt forced by necessity to say humbly, "Master, please strike me on the right temple in the future

4

because I now have completely lost the hearing in my left ear." Stunned by such patience, Marino then mitigated the indiscreet severity of his discipline.'[11]

Consequently Marino would now moderate his own severity through the test of Romuald's humility. He realized that the moral stature of this youth who was with him for only a short while, was anything but mediocre, and that love could do much more than the rod. These two remained together for about three years.

One day, perhaps in 978, some emissaries of Doge Peter Orseolo I of Venice came to the hermitage. They had come in person to say that Marino and Romuald were expected at the palace because the Doge wished urgently to speak with them. They had been preceded there by 'a venerable abbot, Guarino' from the monastery of Saint Michael of Cuxa,[12] returning from a pilgrimage to the Holy Land. Doge Peter considered these three as men of God and had called them together for counsel about his decision to renounce his dukedom and the goods of his property, and to abandon his family in order to become a monk. Peter Damian affirms that this decision was the consequence of a 'stroke of divine grace and the sincere contrition of Peter'[13] for having backed a conspiracy against Peter Candino, his predecessor as Doge who was murdered in order to gain the dukedom. Hearing the Doge's confession, the three believed they saw the sign of a real conversion and, in his resolution to become a monk, the best way to amend for the crime. Supported by the favorable opinion of these servants of the Lord, Peter Orseolo that same night 'along with his servant, one John Gradenigo . . . and the three blessed men mentioned above, sought refuge in Gaul at Abbot Gurarino's monastery,'[14] namely, at Cuxa in the eastern Pyrenees region.

The five settled down this way: Peter and John became monks in the retinue of Guarino at Cuxa; Marino and Romuald built themselves a humble hermitage in the vicinity, consistent with their eremitical ways. Things remained this way for a year, then Peter and John reunited with Marino and Romuald.[15] The fervor animating the

Saint Apollinare in Classe at Ravenna

From Mittarelli-Costadoni, Annales Camaldulenses, T. VII. Venice 1762

four hermits helped give their spiritual progress a decisive thrust. Romuald stood out and, to quote Peter Damian, 'he moved wondrously from one virtue to another with burning, heartfelt longing, and outdistanced by far the other brethren'[16] so that, beginning with Marino, all of them asked Romuald to be their father and superior. They alternated their rhythms of prayer with those of working the land where they lived, then increased their fasting and personal deprivations.[17]

The first community of the 'Romualdian' mold was born without any of the planning or foresight of our own organized ethics to which we have grown accustomed. This was providential for that level of reform for which the Lord was preparing his servant. One of the gifts which Romuald soon manifested was showing discretion and balance which was always in demand for the practical asceticism of the others sometimes moved beyond basic obedience to God and the precepts of the Rule. But he always asked the most of himself. His biographer writes: 'he did not allow the full fast, *i.e.* spending the entire day without touching any food, to be interpreted as an absolute for the others, even though he himself would often practice it... so he little appreciated one who began great things for a while, then did not persevere.'

He adopted a similar standard for the discipline of vigils, for which he counselled 'moderation and great discretion.' And his teaching regarding prayer was precise: 'If possible, it is better to pray one psalm from the heart and with compunction, than to run through a hundred with a distracted mind.' If someone did not possess such a capacity, however, he exhorted him at least not to despair, nor become lukewarm in recitation, until 'He who had given the good will would also finally grant the ability.'[18] And one who immediately follows such instructions preserves all the wise inspiration of him who is no longer in the first steps of faith's journey, but already savors the joy of lived experience. He said, 'Once the mind's intention is fixed on God, God would watch over prayer's fragrance which can be disturbed by the winds of external passing thoughts. Indeed, involuntary thoughts are not too worrisome where there is right intention.'[19] Later on this humane and balanced method of his would earn Romuald the epithet 'Father of the sensible hermits who live according to the Rule.'[20]

We do not know how long Romuald remained at Cuxa. We do know that one day he felt forced to abandon the hermitage in the Pyrenees and hasten to Ravenna in order to console his father Sergio who had become a monk at Saint Severus, but was now having second thoughts and at the point of returning to the world. His son's arrival and persuasive work restored his peace.[21]

A little before Romuald's precipitous departure, the ex-Doge Peter Orseolo 'had happily ended his days' with a holy death. And the little eremitical nucleus broke apart: Guarino, John Gradenigo and Marino turned toward Montecassino, but not much later Marino continued alone toward Apulia where it appears he died at the hands of thieves.[22]

His father's crisis fortunately over, Romuald took up the eremitical way once again, establishing himself in the environs of Ravenna, near Ponte di Pietro. However, he did not stay long in that swampy climate. He was forced to move near a little church called Saint Martin in the Woods[23] which belonged to the monastery of Classe. This second eremitical phase presents new aspects of Romuald's life. He made further strides in spiritual experience, to which the Cuxa period had decisively contributed, enriched also by the presence and fervor of the other hermits mentioned earlier. It is of this point in the saint's life that Peter Damian comments: 'Used to the struggle and strengthened by this time, Christ's soldier learned to climb higher summits and grow stronger every day. He became ever-stronger, so he no longer feared the tricks of the weakened enemy.'[24]

The allusion to tricks of the Evil One has its foundation in a customary event in the lives of the saints: temptation by the spirit of evil, allowed by God, which proves their faithfulness, purifies them of pride and disposes them for even higher gifts. When the Evil One did not succeed in overcoming Romuald in person, he used to agitate his disciples' souls against him or against anyone who respected him.[25] We have the example of what happened to him near Bagno di Romagna where the saint had built a monastery. He was actually beaten and driven away by his own brethren because Romuald had set aside for other monks needier than themselves a sum of money which he had received as a gift from the Marquis of Tuscany.[26] Such a tremendous desolation entered the soul of God's servant that he swore to himself he would never again take an interest in others, but only think of his own salvation. But he soon reconsidered and rejected this evil suggestion, continuing on his way.[27]

At this stage in his account, Peter Damian places Romuald 'not far from Mount Catria.'[28] The saint's presence in the Catria environs has suggested to almost all historians the belief that he had founded, or at least given a markedly eremitical stamp to, the Hermitage of Fonte Avellana, so famous in monastic and Italian ecclesiastical history, and still occupied by Camaldolese today.[29]

Then there is mention that the man of God spent time as a recluse[30] near the marshes of Comacchio, perhaps near the monastery of Saint Mary in Aula Regia (or in Auregario);[31] and then in Perio, the present-day Saint Albert's, fifteen kilometers northeast of Ravenna.[32]

The Pereo period is another significant time in Saint Romuald's life. The events there described by Peter Damian lead us to suppose that our saint had spent one of his longer intervals here. As at Cuxa, he found himself the head of another nucleus of brethren who shared the eremitical life with him. We know the names of some of them, while others are referred to in very interesting episodes underlining in a remarkable way the course of the Romualdian reform. These are their names: William, Bruno Boniface, John and Benedict. The first is mentioned only once, but we will meet the other three again when, through a series of circumstances, they will become protagonists with Master

Romuald in a unique historical moment which will fashion them, in life and in writings, more credible interpreters of his teaching.

An unforeseen event occurs in this time. One day at sunset, the young Emperor Otto III[33] arrived at the hermitage unexpectedly. The monarch felt the urgent need to consult with Romuald both because the situation at Classe had not improved regarding its observance of the Rule and because those monks wanted to have Romuald back again—as abbot! Besides informing the saint of the coming election, Otto also came to press for his acceptance. Meanwhile, night had fallen and the saint took time to pray. Then he said he would prepare things for the Emperor's rest. Unprepared for visitors, he gave his own sleeping pallet to his illustrious guest who adjusted it to himself, but found the blanket unbearably bristly. Their discussion continued the next morning at the palace where the Emperor finding Romuald firm in refusing election, felt obliged to threaten him with excommunication through a regional synod of bishops. At this point the holy hermit had to surrender 'and was forced to take on the governing of souls.'[34]

The quarrels were not long in coming. Instead of facilitating the respect and obedience of the monks, the holy abbot's gentle and upright character suddenly found itself countering the lack of discipline and the minimal obligation to which the monks had grown accustomed. Still, the servant of God who took seriously the obligations undertaken before God and his own conscience, did not feel intimidated and 'governed the monks under the strict discipline of the Rule and no one was permitted to deviate without punishment. With his mind's eye fixed on heaven, he was not afraid to displease men by obeying God.'[35] Obviously, the two views of life did not agree and the monks, now unable to oppose their abbot's upright position, began 'to attack him with much underhanded murmuring and prick him with the tough thorns of scandals.'[36] The tense atmosphere and bitter invective in the house which contrasted with the patient work of the servant of the

Lord, ended by being perilous in his own journey to holiness, so he decided to go to the Emperor and Archbishop of Ravenna and tender his resignation.[37] He had to travel as far as Tivoli to meet with the Emperor who was laying siege to that rebellious city where his captain, one Mazzolino, had been killed. Romuald threw down his pastoral staff in front of the Emperor and resigned.[38] Otto was quite saddened by this event, but had to agree. The year was 999.

Romuald's presence in Tivoli was providential. With true Christian spirit, he charged Otto and the people of Tivoli with bloody dissension and began making peace between the two factions. Accounting for the reasons for the rivalry, he succeeded in lessening the mutual hatred and had them agree to these conditions: Tivoli would knock down part of its city wall, deliver some hostages, and send the murderer of the Emperor's official in chains to ask pardon from the murdered man's mother. Meanwhile, the holy abbot had convinced the woman to grant the murderer pardon, and he returned unharmed and reconciled.[39]

Romuald knew a holy hermit named Venerio who lived the solitary life not far from the city, but who had not received an obedience from any abbot. Our saint urged him to obtain permission from his superior and follow his plan peacefully.[40] Then, still at Tivoli, Romuald managed to convert a young German named Tammo who was a very close friend and advisor to the Emperor. He had previously committed perjury and had been the indirect cause for the murder of Crescenzio, a Roman senator. He repented and confessed the deed, deciding to join the saint's retinue and become a monk.[41]

The foregoing gives a clear enough picture of the relationship between Romuald and Otto III. We should add that the saint's esteem for the young monarch and Otto's own veneration for the man of God created the conditions for a profound friendship. So the holy abbot found himself often in the capacity of imperial advisor with free access to the court. Possessing a profound religious sense, Otto had known the younger Romuald at Ravenna, or more exactly, at Pereo, around 998. The casualness with which he accepted sleeping on the holy hermit's pallet, just like the frankness with which the saint renounced his pastoral service in Classe, reveal a familiarity between the two, trust and moral influence proving beneficial for both. Peter Damian explicitly writes that it is due to this friendship that Otto always shows himself 'more benevolent toward the monastic order and religiously sympathetic toward the servants of God.'[42] As for Romuald, friend and father (understood in a more genuine sense of the word), loyal to authority but never an obsequious flatterer, he desired and learned how to keep his freedom of speech and action. He did not hesitate to call the monarch to task for breaking his oath to protect the life of the rebellious Crescenzio, and sent him on pilgrimage to Saint Michael-on-Gargano in expiation. Otto obeyed, going from Rome to that holy place, barefoot.[43]

Otto had indicated to Romuald his intention 'to leave his reign and assume the monastic habit.'[44] Presumably he would have done so, if death had not cut him down at the age of twenty–three, after a serious illness. The strong and fascinating personality of the holy hermit could only make a profound impression on the imperial court. Some of the courtiers would come to choose the Lord's service, as we will soon see, placing themselves at the school of Romuald whose history is about to open on one of its most beautiful chapters, rich in content.

When the Emperor left on his pilgrimage, Romuald went to Montecassino. Very attentive to the more authentic symbols of tradition, he had to realize his desire to go there to venerate the tomb of Saint Benedict, father of western monasticism, as though going to the very source of monastic experience. Tammo, Boniface and other German converts accompanied him.[45] Tammo has been mentioned already. Later, we will speak of Boniface at length because circumstances create there a person of the first order in discipleship and the Romualdian reform.

At Montecassino our saint could again see his dear disciple John Gradenigo who had lived the eremitical life for some years in the area of the ancient abbey, venerated for its history and sanctity.[46] Disciples had gathered around John, one of whom would become distinguished among the Romualdians: Benedict of Benevento, a passionate young man who placed himself in Romuald's company once he had come to know him. He was a monk from the monastery of Holy Savior near his city, and had received permission from his abbot to become a hermit. Now he was separating from John who had told him about abbot Romuald. 'Old John, ever the devoted upholder of humility, had taught Benedict while on his road to recovery. He had acknowledged that all those counsels of life and heavenly words he had suggested had been obtained from the sanctity of Master Romuald. This Romuald, he said, outstanding in our day, lived not out of presumption but along the lines of the hermitage Collections of the Fathers in great humility with beautiful and sublime practices, and he taught us the truly correct path. Young Benedict used to become kindled when listening to John praise Master Romuald so often as the father of the sensible hermits who lived under the Rule.' John said these and other edifying things, and his words sank deeply into the thirsty soul of young Benedict until 'as one who had found good luck without searching for it, he moved out of his dwelling place, got on his horse and hurried off in utter simplicity to search for Romuald. Once he found him, no one could ever pull him away from Romuald's side.'[47]

Romuald's stay at Montecassino must have extended longer than expected because the holy man contracted a serious illness, to the point of death. He recovered, and as soon as he could, headed for Pereo, accompanied still by Tammo, Boniface and Benedict. It is likely that other disciples joined them at Pereo, as Saint Peter Damian mentions.[48] Besides devoting themselves to incessant prayer, vigils and various ascetical practices, the holy hermits worked for their sustenance. One made spoons and vessels, another spun wool, still another wove nets for the many fishermen in and about the Comacchio valley.[49] For more details, we must now refer to the aforementioned Bruno of Querfurt (or Bruno Boniface), 'a celebrated figure who today is honored by the Russian Church for being one of its blessed martyrs.'[50]

He became acquainted with Romuald at the monastery of Saint Alexis-on-the-Aventine in Rome, where Otto III had lived upon returning from Poland. Young Bruno held the office of court chaplain. He was born in 974, the son of Bruno and Ida, Count and Countess of Querfurt in Saxony. The family had married into the imperial house of Weimar Saxony, in other words: The Ottos.[51] He studied in the cathedral school of Magdeburg, was ordained priest and became a canon of the same cathedral. Saint Peter Damian says that 'he was well educated in the liberal arts, renowned above all for his study of music and chant.'[52] Bruno was very close to the Emperor, who would often refer to him as 'My soul.' His acquaintance with Romuald gave the young German priest a new direction which kept him at the holy abbot's side from then onwards, absorbing his teaching more than anyone else. He resigned his imperial appointment and became a monk.

One day while passing the church of Saint Boniface the martyr,[53] his contemporary, he pondered: "I am also named Boniface—should I not also be Christ's martyr?"[54] He realized that something new had just been given life in his heart: his decision to become a monk and his desire to suffer martyrdom became the essential components of his life. It was as though Providence were drawing him to the school of Romuald; first on the road to the hermitage, then towards martyrdom.

Together with Tammo and others from the court, Bruno Boniface started his first period of eremitical life in a hermitage which Romuald had opened near Rome.[55] Here 'their studies of Christian philosophy began to bloom and the brothers' hearts greened beneath the rain of the Holy Spirit, producing blossoms of virtue and fruits of holiness in the fear of God.'[56]

However, it was not long before a series of political events convinced Romuald and his disciples to return to Pereo. For greater security, Otto III moved to Ravenna, permitting more frequent contacts with the Pereo hermits.

One day the Emperor visited with a particular intent which held surprising novelty for the small group of ascetics. King Boleslaw of Poland had requested from Otto some missionaries to evangelize the eastern section of his kingdom, as far as the border with the Kiev territories (western Russia). The area was inhabited by some tribes (the Piecinghi, or Peceneghi) who were 'the most savage of all the pagan peoples.'[57] To be honest, Otto appears to have had a hand in mediating Boleslaw's request of Romuald because, even though he was supporting it strictly from a religious angle, he was also concerned with certain political projects of his own. Apart from this secondary motive, the monarch's intervention was sincere and urgent. From their point of view, Romuald and his disciples considered the proposal only from the perspective of Gospel service and agreed to it, convinced that it was God's will.

Romuald, already known for his prophetic intuition, probably would have pressed the case further, perceiving within the evangelization of unbelievers the most expressive moment of a life devoted to Christ in the monastic and eremitical spheres, as if it were their natural conclusion. What Otto now made him foresee seemed to correspond with what he had already considered many times in his heart. The Emperor said to him with conviction: "The brethren would build a monastery in some beautiful woods over there, offering them a good retreat on Christian soil at the border of the pagan lands. Then they who are seeking the Lord's way would have a threefold advantage: the hoped-for cenobium for the novices coming from the world; the precious solitude of the hermitage for the mature monks thirsting for God; and the evangelization of pagans for those who finally yearn to choose to be with Christ."[58]

At this, Romuald's face became radiant. He envisioned now the essential form for the entire program of his monastic reform with that 'initial training of the cenobium, the perfecting of the hermitage, and the apostolate of martyrdom.'[59] Nevertheless, he preferred the father's balance to the superior's authority: 'He did not want to impose the mission on any of his disciples through a superior's authority, but gave all the brethren the freedom to stay or go, leaving the decision to each of them.'[60] Peter Damian is clear that the issue was of such importance for Romuald that he did not want to decide without the certainty of God's will. He turned to God in secret and, before Otto returned to Ravenna, three of his disciples had declared themselves ready to depart. They were: Boniface, 'whose way of life by far surpassed all the others,'[61] Benedict of Benevento, and John, formerly a monk of Classe who was humble and always joyful, dearest to the holy abbot .

Benedict and John set out for Poland in autumn, 1001, while Bruno Boniface went to Rome to obtain faculties to preach. While there, he was also ordained archbishop 'to the nations.' Then early in 1003 he too set out in the direction of Poland. Benedict and John had already presented themselves before Boleslaw, wishing that Bruno could have joined them beforehand, and they began their apostolic work.

The king personally took care that a hermitage was built for them. It was erected near Casimiria, where three young Polish men—Matthew, Isaac and Christian—joined them a little later. All seemed hopeful for the little hermitage until one night some pagans from nearby broke into the cloister, convinced that the humble hermits were watching over a treasure for the king. They murdered all five. As for the treasure, of course they found nothing. John and Benedict were the first to die, then Matthew and Isaac, and finally Christian. 'Matthew was lying near the church; Christian was stretched out in the middle of the square; Isaac was stretched out as if begging mercy, struck three times; John had fallen from his bed to the ground and seemed to be praying on his knees; only Benedict, the leader of the holy group, was lying as though asleep, having given his soul to God with a glorious death.'[62] It was November 10, 1002.

16

And where was Bruno Boniface? We have seen that he could only set out for Poland from Rome at the beginning of 1003, with plans to join John and Benedict. Crossing Italy's border by river, he entered Hungary on the Danube. Ignorant of the events at the Casimiria hermitage, he decided to investigate the pagan area of the Black Hungarians, engaging in missionary endeavors. In this he was not very successful, so he thought it wise to quicken the pace of his journey to Poland. He crossed the Carpathians, and entered the duchy of Kiev, proclaiming the Gospel to the Peceneghi on the coast of the Black Sea, with happier results than among the Hungarians. Seeing this mission thrive, he went back into Poland eager to join his brethren. He contacted Boleslaw as soon as he could, who appraised him of the events, telling him with profound grief what fate had dealt John, Benedict, and the others. His dismay added ardor to Bruno's desire to pour out his own blood too, in witness to Christ. Deciding to write their 'passion' in the meantime, he went to the place of martyrdom and asked the faithful for the basic information.[63]

In 1008 Boniface told Boleslaw that he intended to return to Prussia or Belorussia in the area formed by the Vistula and Niemen rivers, and a little later he established himself there. The Lord blessed his preaching with a great number of converts. Peter Damian himself underscores the efficacy of Boniface's holy zeal: 'When the venerable man joined the king of Prussia, he insisted on preaching ardently with force of soul.'[64]

Moved by his love for Christ, he turned toward the Jadringhi tribe of Sudawa on the Prusso-Lithuanian border. He met hostile resistance here from the king of that territory who realized what the presence and work of the holy archbishop represented, and cut short all Boniface's good intentions, forcing him to undergo the 'proof of fire'[65] before he would give him permission to preach. Two stacks of wood facing one another were prepared and the fire was lit. Boniface put on the episcopal insignia and walked down the middle unharmed. The 'judgment of God' was favorably interpreted for the holy bishop and the king himself requested baptism, followed by a large proportion of the population. The king's brother, however, was one who remained outside grace. Boniface later tried to persuade him. Furious, the recalcitrant prince's only response was to arrest the bishop and order him beheaded. It was March 9, 1009. Bruno Boniface had worked in Prussian territory for only two months. In the bloom of his thirty-five years, he had confirmed in blood his faith in Christ, as had his five holy brothers.

The martyrdoms of Romuald's disciples are not beyond the scope of these remarks. In Peter Damian's reflection at the end of chapter 27 in *Vita Romualdi*, he tells of Bruno Boniface, in a digression which usefully reflects upon Romuald himself. 'We tried to give here briefly a mention of him (Boniface) and the other disciples of Romuald to show with their praise how great was their master; that way, while the excellence of scholars resonates in the ears of the faithful, it is apparent how noble was their master from that same school which he directed.'[66]

Formed and raised, then, at this school where the ascetical disciplines had in Romuald not simply a teacher of profound experience, but also a model to imitate, these disciples, 'soldiers in the cenobium, experts in the hermitage, heroes in the apostolate,'[67] wrote on this margin of Europe, Christianized through their martyrdom, one of the most beautiful pages in the history of Romuald and the Camaldolese.[68]

Meanwhile, new chapters were opening up for Romuald. The sources at this point inform us of his presence in Istria. What is he doing in Istria? A single answer cannot be found in the historical sources. It remains conjecture, but the most plausible explanation is that he may have been yearning to spread his reform in new areas, with new monastic centers. We assume that monastic reform, with particular attention to the then fashionable enough phenomenon of eremiticism, would always be his great longing. So, it is not arbitrary to tie together his frequent shifts to such an undertaking.

Saint Peter Damian brings us back to this idea when he speaks of Romuald as 'impatient with fruitlessness, eager where he could find the right land for producing a harvest of souls...' [69] And again: 'Such a tremendous ardor for bearing good fruit glowed in the holy man's heart that he was never content with what he had done; while he was doing one thing, he would hurry so that he could begin work on another, so much so that one might have thought he wanted to transform the whole world into a hermitage and to have all people join the monastic order.' [70]

Romuald established himself at Parenzo where he stayed three years during which, besides performing his reform work, he applied himself to further spiritual progress, accompanied by some mystical manifestations. Peter Damian writes that Romuald had built a monastery during the first year at Parenzo, but lived as a recluse [71] for the other two years, setting himself up in a more complete retreat and dedicating himself exclusively to contemplation. 'There divine goodness raised him up to the summit of perfection, so that he penetrated many hidden mysteries of the Old and New Testaments with the light of intelligence and, inspired by the Holy Spirit, foresaw many future events. Sometimes he worried about his yearning to melt into tears, but no matter what he might do, he did not succeed in attaining perfect compunction of heart.

But one day while he sang psalms in his cell, he ran across this verse of Psalm 31,8: *I will give you intelligence and I will teach you the way you should go; I will watch over you.* Suddenly there came such an outpouring of tears and his mind was so illumined to understand the sense of divine Scripture that from then on, for as long as he lived and anytime he wished, copious tears would easily spout, and many mystical things in the Scriptures were no longer hidden from him. The contemplation of God often seized him so that, bursting into tears and inflamed with an ineffable ardor of divine love, he would shout out: *Dear Jesu, my sweet honey, ineffable longing, sweetness of the saints, gentleness of the angels,* and other similar expressions.

But the things he uttered in joy we are unable to express in human language. As the Apostle says, *We do not know how we should pray, but the Spirit himself prays through us with unspeakable groanings* (Rm. 8,26).'[72]

Romuald's fame had been spreading for some time, particularly engaging the monastic and ecclesiastical worlds in general. Monks and churchmen spoke of his holiness and the charisms which the Lord had given him, and many turned to him for advice. They called him 'Master Romuald' or 'Abbot Romuald.' Thus we find some monks of Biforco[73] coming to Parenzo, needing advice about eremitical life, as well as other seekers needing advice about the ascetical life. The saint satisfied their requests and promised to write for them a 'small book on how to fight the Evil One.'[74] He also let them understand that he would join them at Biforco.

Even if he kept this promise, he did not stay long at Biforco, probably because of the poor reception these monks gave his advice, particularly regarding poverty. So he departed and travelled to the Marches region near Camerino.[75] An important biographical note explains why the holy abbot made this 'umpteenth' move. 'Impatient with fruitlessness, Romuald began to search with longing for a place where he could find suitable land for producing the harvest of souls.'[76]

He did not have the impatience of one who cannot slow his pace for travel, but the blessedly impatient yearning which does not tolerate useless delays in the search for better situations where one can live to the maximum for God and for the brethren. One such example from the saint's life will come up again when, as we shall see, he will try at least twice to travel the road to Hungary in order to embrace martyrdom.

The holy hermit went near the Marca of Camerino to consult gentlemen of that region. Their joyous welcome with a determination to support him in any way he needed made him realize his reputation had preceded him. Thanks to God and these good men, Romuald chose a broad valley between Fabriano and Cingoli, dominated on the north end by Mount

Sanvicino (1485 m.), furrowed by the Esino waters. This is Valdicastro, semantically the 'Valley of the Castello' because there was an ancient castle dominating it from above.[77] Adjacent to a small church and a little monastery of nuns—both given to the saint—they had built some wooden cells where he and his disciples lived.

The time Romuald spent in the Camerino area is indicative of the complexity of his reform works which increasingly were concerned not only with monks, but also with simoniacal bishops and priests.[78] Our saint was both courageous and severe with such men, so that some simoniacal clergy even tried to kill him when, advancing their excuse that simony was really not such a serious sin, the man of God reproached them: "Give me the books of Canons and confront your own texts themselves whether what I say is true."[79]

Another rather significant element of this reform was the institution and creation of various small communities of priests willing to live a communal lifestyle in greater poverty and under obedience to a preposito (superior). Lastly, Romuald took an interest in the nuns for whom he founded a monastery in the environs of Valdicastro. The results of these reforming acts must have proved good enough, if Peter Damian expresses it this way: 'Who could express in writing or explain in speech how many harvested souls the Lord gathered through his mediation?'[80]

Many came to him, confessed their sins and distributed their goods to the poor, after receiving the holy hermit's advice. Others decided to become monks. 'The most blessed man was like a seraph because he even glowed incomparably with the flame of divine love and, wherever he would go, he enkindled others with the fire of his holy preaching.'[81] What happened in Camerino and its surroundings was repeated not far from there in the area of Orvieto, where Romuald went after receiving a request from Count Farolfo. He gave the saint some lands where, with the kindness of other people, he built a monastery.[82] The most beautiful flower the holy abbot could gather from the area of Orvieto was Guido, an innocent youth who, becoming a monk in the school of Romuald, gave signs of authentic sanctity and died very young.[83]

At this point in our account, another chapter full of meaning opens up in the life of a man who, even if professing the hermit life, showed himself most attentive to the greater problems in the Church of his day. One gets the impression that the Italian lands simply were no longer enough for him. He had received the news of the martyrdom of his most beloved disciple Bruno Boniface in distant Russia. His desire also to give his life for Christ gradually assumed greater dimensions as the days passed by. He thought about Hungary and began preparations for his departure with the quickness of a more animated zeal. His first concern was to obtain the Apostolic See's necessary permission to preach. While getting the license, two of his disciples named Ingelbert and Gregory were consecrated bishops, and at least twenty four others of his monks announced themselves ready to follow him: 'Such a great longing to die for Christ burned in them all that the holy man found it difficult to depart for this undertaking with only a few.'[84]

The band of missionary-monks journeyed with Romuald towards the regions of the Hungarians, people of Finnic stock, barbaric customs and pagan religions. The saint and his brethren entered Carinzia across the Friuli from Ravenna, but already a difficult trial awaited the man of God. A strange illness seized him: his face swelled; his stomach repelled food; and a persistent fever sapped all his energy. His hoped-for recovery did not appear imminent, so he decided to return to Italy against his own will, because he did not wish to sacrifice further his anxious monks' yearning to reach their mission field. In less time than one would think, every symptom of illness vanished, the fever was contained and his strength returned. Without giving it a second thought, he turned his back on Italy and took up once again the road to Hungary. But again, unexpectedly, the same sickness returned: the same symptoms and the same effects. Romuald wanted to understand better; he prayed and called together the brethren, saying: "I understand it is not God's will that I go abroad. But because I know well your hearts' desire, I do not want to force any of you to turn back. Even before us, many tried with all their strength to attain the victory of martyrdom, but since Divine Providence willed otherwise, they were compelled to remain in their situation. Even if I were sure that none of you would attain martyrdom, still I want each to choose either to go forward or return with me." [85] Seven returned with him, twenty-two remained, and two went elsewhere. But no one attained martyrdom.

Upon his return, Romuald once again went to Orvieto, then towards Perugia he entered Sienese territory where he founded the monastery of Martignana near the Val d'Elsa hill. Then he went again to Classe and finally, to Parenzo in Istria. Here the man of God intended to stay for a good length of time, until a diplomatic mission of Pope Sergius IV begged him (and if he refused, commanded him) to return quickly to Italy. He obeyed promptly and left for that place which was always particularly dear to him. 'In this way, Italy, his pupil, was once again able to recover its master.'[86] Once he reached Italian soil and was reinvigorated by the Pope's wishes which greatly encouraged him in his undertakings, our saint was quick to resume the familiar rhythms of the itinerant monk.

He turned toward central Italy. He went to Saint Vincent at Furlo by the Flaminia road. In the surrounding area he directed the construction of the Pietralata hermitage, then again a shift to Valdicastro, then to Acquabella on the Umbrian-Marchigiano Apennine range where he directed another small hermitage. Finally he went to Sitria. 'Everywhere he went, he always bore fruit, always accumulated more souls, uprooting men from the world. As though he were totally transformed in fire, he enkindled the souls of throngs toward heavenly desires.'[87]

Several miraculous signs also blossomed. A beech tree which, ripe for cutting because it was bulky, fell in the direction opposite to which it was hanging, because the servant of God made a simple sign of the cross. A woodcutter remained unharmed through Romuald's prayer when he was knocked down by an oak tree. A priest was cured of a terrible toothache simply by a finger's touch. In all of this, good and simple people perceived the epiphany of God's goodness working through his faithful servant with signs of consolation: "We give thanks, almighty God," they exclaimed, "that you consider our region worthy of illumination by the splendor of so brilliant a heavenly body. A true angel of God, authentic holy prophet, and great light hidden from the world has appeared in our land!" [88]

Still, there were ever-present trials and sufferings for Romuald, caused by some of his less sincere monks—some significant stations along this *via dolorosa*, like Classe, Verghereto, Valdicastro and Sitria, as we shall soon see. They show us how hours of darkness accompany the joys of contemplation and fruits of a good harvest. Romuald knew one of these darker moments at Sitria[89] not far from Mount Catria, on the boundary between Umbria and the Marches where we find him coming from Acquabella. The Sitria period is unique among the more significant times in the life of this servant of Christ. Indeed, a whole set of circumstances in which intense moral sufferings interweave with moments of ineffable spiritual joy, leads us to believe that Romuald came here at the summit of his faith's maturation, touching now the mystical heights through a wonderful consonance amid charisms of seraphic love, the highest contemplation, prophecy, the gift of tears, and an intelligence penetrating the Word of God.

But before tasting the rapture of the heights, he had to touch the depths of bitterness, causing him the degradation of disgraceful calumny. He found a monk named Roman living at Sitria, born a nobleman, one whom Peter Damian does not hesitate to describe as 'absolutely, habitually degenerate.'[90] Obviously Abbot Romuald felt obliged to reprove him many times for his dissolute conduct, even to the point of subjecting him to corporal punishments. But one time poor Roman, overwhelmed by a demonic spirit out for revenge, directly accused the man of God of the same shameful immorality, insolently denouncing him in front of all the other brethren. Anger and indignation upset the venerable old saint. It was decided unanimously to excommunicate Romuald according to the Rule.[91] Beyond mere separation, he was thrown into prison and deprived of the celebration of Mass.[92]

Romuald felt no need to defend himself. Silent, with head bowed, he submitted to the unjust command, 'accepting good–naturedly this unjust imposition. He observed the penance as if he really were guilty and did not try to approach the sacred altar for almost six months.'[93] He was strengthened by thinking about the crucified Christ, the spotless lamb who was, without a whimper, abandoned into executioners' hands. Then he understood that he had been asked to be a holocaust for that disgraceful moral lynching and so, live in his flesh the kind of grain of wheat which, fallen to the ground, is subjected to decay in order to bear the fruit of grain with its promise of bread.

But we are amazed and ask ourselves how those monks who had the examples of irreproachable conduct of their abbot and master before their very eyes could so easily have believed the lie and had judged him so superficially. Peter Damian himself makes this observation: 'What is more amazing, above all, is that such spiritual men could have believed such wickedness in a decrepit old man... when even if he had not lacked the will, nature itself and the frigidity of an exhausted body would have prevented the possibility. But we must believe that such a repugnant trial came to him as God's will to increase the holy man's merits.'[94] But like the Lord whose hand is merciful, Romuald transformed that time of darkness into dawning light.

One day, while the saint was immersed in deep contemplation, he discerned the sign of an explicit command coming from God: an injunction to cease his acquiescent attitude and freely resume the celebration of the Holy Mysteries. He obeyed, but not without letting his monks know what his soul had clearly perceived. Here is what Peter Damian writes: 'Resuming the celebration of the sacred mysteries the next day, he was rapt in ecstasy as he came to the second Secret prayer of the Mass (*i.e.* the Eucharistic Prayer), and he stayed silent for so long that those present stood amazed. Asked later why he would delay such an unusually long time during the sacrifice of the Mass, he answered, "I was swept into heaven and presented before God, and suddenly a divine voice commanded me to explain the Psalms through this understanding God was giving me, then to write it down according to my own meager intelligence. Then pressed by such tremendous ineffable terror, I could only respond: fiat, fiat." Indeed, the holy man later explained clearly the entire Psalter and some prophetic canticles. Although the rules of grammar were lacking, the overall sense was perfect.'[95]

As for poor Roman, not even this example of the holy master could induce him to repent. He worsened, and a little later left Sitria, intrigued to obtain the episcopate of Nocera Umbra through simony, and two years later, 'meeting with divine justice, he lost it, along with his life.'[96]

Romuald meanwhile, enriched by 'the gift of wisdom descending from above,' set about making up for whatever evil had spread among the friends of his disciples, with the firm conviction that 'a harvest of justice is sown in peace for the peacemakers.'[97] Peace returned and with it, the esteem and veneration of his disciples towards their holy master. One day they asked him: "Master, what sort of age does a soul have, or in what form is it presented before God's presence?" He answered: "I know a man in Christ whose soul was brought before God, splendid as snow, appearing as a human in the prime of life." Somewhat satisfied, they still wished to know more, so they asked him who that man was. Romuald changed the subject and would not say more about the matter, 'but the disciples attributed this reference to himself...they realized he was that very man.'[98]

At Sitria, then, Romuald returned to living with great fervor. The monks and even the valley's families and pastors engaged in a holy rivalry in various ascetical practices of a rather rigorous nature, so that Peter Damian exclaims: 'O golden century of Romuald which, although it did not know the torments of the persecutions, still did not lack a voluntary martyrdom! I say *golden age* because it nurtured among the wilds of the mountains and forests such citizens of the heavenly Jerusalem.'[99]

The holy abbot lived as a recluse there for about seven years, maintaining an almost uninterrupted silence, 'keeping his tongue quiet while preaching with his life, as though he could never work for the conversion of souls more than that way.'[100] During an entire Lenten season he limited his regime for a month and a half to a handful of boiled chick-peas and a little porridge with wild grasses each day. And he wore three hairshirts against his bare flesh. God also showed mercy toward the sick monks and faithful at Sitria through Romuald's prayer and sanctity. The sick regained their health simply by eating a piece of bread blessed by Romuald.

After seven years at Sitria, Romuald received some messengers from Emperor Henry II. Romuald's friendship with Henry's cousin, Otto III, and his widespread fame kindled a very strong desire to meet and know the saint.[101] The good monarch who was a friend and fair judge of monks, did not miss an opportunity to grant them favors and protection. The state in which the Emperor had found the Abbey of the Holy Savior on-the-Amiata[102] where Abbot Guinizo was not up to the task of governing the monks, precipitated his decision to meet Romuald the holy reformer, and name him as replacement. For his part, Romuald found it necessary to search for other places to house some of his disciples since so many had thronged to the solitude of Sitria.

Although he respectfully appreciated the imperial messengers who had invited him to the palace, Romuald had the messengers understand that he preferred to postpone the meeting because he had been in silence for such a long time. His monks intervened: "Master, you can see that we your followers are now so many that we can no longer all live here together easily. So go, please, and ask the emperor for some large monastery in which to locate this crowd of your followers." The saint seemed not to give much weight to their insistence and assured them calmly, in a prophetical way, "You will receive as a gift from the king the monastery of Mount Amiata; so now give some consideration as to who should be abbot there."[103] After a moment in reflection, he followed the emperor's messengers.

Henry set off for the meeting and, upon seeing the holy hermit, exclaimed with all due respect: "If only God granted my soul to be in your body!" But humble and serene Romuald did not venture to break his silence. He decided to speak the next day, however, and with mythic power, demanded that the emperor restore the rights of some churches, asked him to take care of the poor against the oppression of the powerful, and requested a monastery for his monks. Longing for nothing better, Henry seized upon this last request and gave the saint the monastery of Amiata, entreating Romuald himself to be the abbot.[104] As he had foreseen, it would not be an easy abbatial tenure. Promoted by other intolerant monks, Guinizo provided all kinds of trials which the man of God endured with wonderful patience, but without deviating from his line of direction. Consistent with his reform ideal, he built a hermitage on the northern slope of Amiata in a large valley through which the Vivo stream flows (a tributary of the Orcia River).[105]

We are now in the year 1023. Romuald is seventy–one years old. But his journey is still not finished. Longing still to be useful to the Church, he returned to the road in search of other areas for new accomplishments. He travelled from Amiata towards the central Tuscan Apennines. He reached Siena and Arezzo, advanced to the large Casentino valley and climbed toward Giogana (1250 m.). He was at Camaldoli.

Since Peter Damian's *Life of Romuald* is silent on the entire matter of Camaldoli's founding, we need to look to other reliable sources, which we will do in the next chapter. So, picking up the trail given us by Saint Peter Damian, we follow our saint now to Valdicastro, the last stage of his earthly sojourn.

This is the third time Romuald has come to Valdicastro and he seems to know the reason for this visit. In fact, Peter Damian writes: 'Romuald returned to the monastery he had built at Valdicastro, feeling now that he was near the end. Awaiting the approach of death with certainty, he built himself a cell with an oratory in order to take reclusion in silence until death. Twenty years earlier, he had predicted to his disciples that he must die in that monastery.'[106] Romuald's motive for returning to Valdicastro is precisely his clear perception that his declining strength signalled the approaching day for his return to the Father. He returned to Valdicastro, built himself a cell a fair distance from the monastery, and retired there in silence. The infirmities and sickness of old age had bent him over, and now a persistent wheezing with an obstinate cough would not allow him the rest he needed. He still followed his usual rhythms of life without mitigating his fasts and vigils.

But one day his strength collapsed and his breathing grew labored. 'As the sun was setting, he asked the brethren helping him to go outside and return to him at daybreak for the celebration of lauds. But they did not immediately go to sleep because they were apprehensive about his approaching death. They were anxious that the master was going to die, so they hid near the cell as though guarding some precious treasure. After some time of listening intently and not hearing any movement or sound, they suspected that he really had died. They knocked on the door and entered quickly. Lighting a flame, they discovered the saint's body lying supine. His blessed soul had already been taken to heaven. He lay there like a celestial pearl, uncared for, but soon to be placed more honorably in the Most High King's treasury. He had died just as he had predicted and he passed on to that place for which he had hoped.'[107] It was June 19, 1027.[108]

This Gospel servant's death was like his life, bearing the sign of an extraordinarily strong moral character in harmony with an entire lifestyle. In his *De Vita Solitaria*, Petrarch has written: *'As he had served Christ through solitude, he returned to Christ from solitude to ask for the reward of his service.'* [109] The words with which Peter Damian ends the story of his hero's life take on for us a greater importance: 'Now he shines among the living stones of the heavenly Jerusalem and exults with the glowing throngs of blessed spirits, vested in the whitest stole of immortality and crowned forever with a glittering crown by the King of kings himself.' [110]

He was buried in the center of the church of Valdicastro, in the earth. Five years later, the Apostolic See gave the monks permission to build an altar over his tomb, [111] which at that time amounted to official recognition of the cult which the faithful had already developed around the saint. This was, for all practical purposes, an authentic and proper canonization. When they exhumed him, the holy body was almost intact. They placed him in a splendid sarcophagus from the Roman epoch, found among the ruins of Tuficum. It is still visible today beneath the altar of the church of Valdicastro.

Romuald's remains stayed there until December 20, 1480. That night in some bizarre, mistaken devotion, two monks wanting to take the precious relics to their own lands, raised the marble lid of the sarcophagus, took out the bones, and tossed them confusedly into a sack which they loaded on a donkey, and fled. They were caught and held in custody at Jesi. The sacred relics were recovered, but a problem regarding their proper destination arose: Jesi, Valdicastro, and Fabriano all demanded possession. There was an argument at once, until Prior General Peter Delfino intervened after arriving from Camaldoli for this set purpose, and succeeded in resolving the dispute. He had recourse to Cardinal Raffaele Riario, Papal legate for the Marches, who decided in favor of Fabriano. The transfer happened on February 6, 1481. The corpse of the blessed man was closed and sealed again in another marble sarcophagus where it is kept today with great veneration. [112]

The sarcophagus of St. Romuald
at the Church of SS. Biagio and Romuald, Fabriano

2. Reflections of a Soul

When we read the Life of Romuald, it is advisable not to dwell on its episodic aspect alone, but also to penetrate the text with a more hermeneutical reading. This helps us to uncover what Peter Damian himself considered much more interesting: Romuald's morality and spirituality.

Getting close to this monk, hermit, reformer, apostle, spiritual director and outstanding churchman, we cannot help being fascinated by his forceful personality. He was hardened to difficulties, generous in giving witness to Christ, extraordinarily full of love and apostolic zeal, blessed with rare charisms which help him reach the highest summits of spiritual joy and intense contemplation. Whoever meets him is immediately impressed by his love for Christ, strong and tender at the same time. He preached to monks and priests, showing himself 'burning' with such powerful love 'that he was like a seraph who glowed incomparably with the flame of divine love; and wherever he would go, he would enkindle others with the fire of his preaching.'[113] He yearned for martyrdom, overwhelmed by a pressing desire to shed his blood for Christ, and to that end embarked on a journey towards Hungary.[114]

He was austere with himself and with others, but showed himself attentive and extraordinarily sensitive.[115] He could count on a strong physique and demanded privations and exertions of himself. Encouraged by his example, many disciples did likewise. Bruno Boniface travelled to Russia as a missionary, walking barefoot in the harsh winter.[116] Sometimes Romuald showed himself severe, but without demonstrating a hardened heart. Still, simoniacal clergy, those living in concubinage, the powerful and the arrogant wealthy ones were terrified[117] of him and trembled before him as if they somehow saw divine retribution in him.[118] He used severe methods with his father, but only to induce him to remain faithful to his monastic profession.[119] Though a seasoned faster, he never imposed his own regimen on others

In fact, he maintained dietary standards which inspire a certain wonder for a man of the century of iron. 'He taught that perfection consisted in eating every day without losing one's hunger.'[120] And he insisted on moderation and discretion for the practice of keeping vigils.

He reached the heights of contemplation, prayed intensely and spoke familiarly with God, yet with his unmistakable sense of equilibrium, counselled that "It is better to pray a psalm from the heart with compunction, if possible, than to run through a hundred psalms with a wandering mind."[121] One should not be disheartened by distractions, he maintained, but pay attention to training one's intention to remain fixed on God.

The rigor with which he disciplined himself did not in any way hinder him from opening up to others. We see him as available and human, familiar, gentle and good with all,[122] so that 'he always appeared cheerful, ever serene.'[123] Having recourse to a vein of good humor helped him repel certain demonic suggestions. God heard him and helped him in healing others possessed by demons—a process which he would mask with healthy irony.[124] Romuald's wit was a weapon against the Evil One, and since he did not want it said that he performed such healings through his own powers, he would pretend to be joking and pass himself off as crazy.[125]

There were many instances of this behavior. Plagued with a ferocious toothache, one monk came to him for help. Romuald opened the window of his cell, breathed on the monk and told the other monks present to do likewise.[126] And he brought back to his senses a man who was out of his mind, by kissing him.[127] Then he cured the monk Gregory of annoying psoriasis simply with a little fresh water.[128] On another occasion, he sent back liberated and refreshed, a thief caught in the act of breaking into the community's meager treasury. He would not apprehend the wrongdoer but only asked him to live more honestly.[129] For all these healing acts, it saddened Romuald to be praised,[130] so much so that he would immediately flee any show of admiration.[131]

Romuald's yearning to live alone with Christ and to die on the cross like Christ burned within him. He was satisfied at Sitria where he climbed the calvary of abusive calumny. He could have defended himself, appealing to the weight of his long experience as a spiritual director and the consistency of his life, but he chose silence and accepted acute humiliation by directing his heart to the gentle lamb Jesu who climbed the steps of the *via dolorosa* without complaint. Certainly it is not right that such wickedness prevailed over justice, but he left to God the time and manner of re-establishing the honesty and innocence of his servant in the eyes of the brethren. The superabundance of grace matured over evil's power by granting Romuald those extraordinary gifts which moved him into God's friendship, establishing him as God's familiar. At the hour of the cross, the burning ecstasy of the seraph allowed him 'to be swept into heaven and presented to God.'[132] He lived immersed in contemplative joy and barely managed to stutter ecstatic expressions of ineffable tenderness: "Dear Jesu, sweet Jesu, Sweetest Honey, Ineffable Longing, Sweetness of the Saints, Gentleness of the Angels."[133] He modulated these expressions and other similar ones like the verses of an Alleluia, singing for joy. He understood what was happening, but did not know how to describe in words what resonated in his heart.[134]

He had the gift of tears and wept out of compunction, in unspeakable tenderness, suddenly and abundantly, while travelling, preaching, celebrating Eucharist, in the secrecy of the cell, and before the brethren. He avoided playing the game of concealment.[135] Through another particular gift of the Spirit 'which dwelled in his heart'[136] he clearly foresaw the circumstances and place of his death twenty years before it happened, and he prepared himself and arranged everything as if for a wedding banquet. He felt so sure, so filled with the power of the Spirit, that he abandoned himself into the arms of Sister Death, without knowing the comfort of the brethren's presence. As he had lived as a solitary, so now alone, he met the Christ who comes.

3. Signs of A Presence

Among the surprises evoked by the story of Saint Romuald's life, there is one embodied in the questions— How could it be that an avowed hermit moved around so much and took such an active interest in problems which might be considered irrelevant to a solitary? With so many complex and multiform activities, how consistent or natural could his vocation to the hermitage have been? Reformer of monasteries, founder of hermitages, counsellor to emperors, the firmest censor of bishops, abbots and priests who lived in concubinage and simony, one concerned about the missionary problem, preacher and spiritual director: all this interlaces attitudes and events which seem to diverge from, rather than confirm, an eremitical line of vision.

And yet, this man of God had a mission (which was anything but secondary) to develop within western monasticism and the Church of his day! Like any Gospel servant, he felt keenly the imperative to be a witness. For Romuald, this became a driving necessity. Just look at the monastic reform, the reorganization and propagation of the eremitical life, and the battle against simony. These clearly define the various areas in which he acted decisively.

How did Romuald arrive at awareness and then at the actualization of these tasks? There is a very enlightened observation we read in the *Life of the Five Brothers:* 'This Romuald, foremost in our days, lived in great humility according to the Collections of the Fathers of the hermitage, not out of his own presumption; he taught us the true way to live.'[137] So the saint conceived his project neither on his own presumption nor on some fanciful whim, but through a mature and lived experience. Recall those first contacts with the very lax and decadent cenobitical environment of Classe, and recall the generous but disappointing eremitical time with Marino—doubtless a holy man, but separated from the context of 'dependence upon an abbot and obedience to a rule.' The period at Cuxa was sufficiently positive, offering Romuald an opportunity to learn and assimilate the doctrine and examples of the Desert Fathers such as Paul, Antony and Hilarion. But reading Cassian's *Spiritual Conferences*[138] seems to have been even more decisive for him.

These circumstances in Romuald's life suggested to him, both in their positive and negative aspects, a project for monastic recovery. He could propose new approaches to the monks, drawing them back to a more responsible fidelity to the Rule which had welcomed them into the life. As for the eremitical phenomenon which though prevalent was without a disciplined framework, Romuald had to realize that the best intentions and sincerity of heart did not always safeguard the hermit from sometimes perilous illusions. Consequently, he became increasingly convinced of the indispensability of certain principles: a Rule, a Community and a Superior. Taken together with the Gospel, these were the only guarantees for the validity of the eremitical option.

Appealing to these principles, Romuald's reforming activities had the sole intent of restoring a minimum structure to the experience of deep Christian worth, never discounting the cardinal criteria of the Benedictine tradition which places obedience to an abbot as one of the fundamentals of monastic life. So, eremitical life, yes, but always watched over by a superior and supported by a community of brethren. The humble dependence of a hermit upon a superior and community, properly understood and respected, saves him from deviations and dangerous inclinations. Such are the characteristics which emerge distinctly from the reform work of the holy abbot who was, after all, generally considered 'the father of sensible hermits who live under a Rule.' And the Rule was none other than the 'mother rule,'[139] the Rule of Saint Benedict. How many times have we asked ourselves how Romuald arrived at his conception of the hermitage!

There are historians, such as Franke[140] and Voigt[141] who say that Romuald was somewhat dependent on eastern monastic institutions, particularly the sixth-century Greeks, but still maintain that he was formed in the eremitical life in north–central Italy (Venice, Pereo, Parenzo), without ever going to the southern region where Greek-rite monastic communities were extant in his day. One historian assumes a reciprocal knowledge between Saint Romuald and Abbot Saint Nilus (+1004), the founder of Grottaferrata,[142] organizer of Greek-rite Basilian cenobitism, and a good friend to Otto III. But this is hypothetical and no historical source confirms it. True or probable as it may well be, such a hypothesis still would not allow us to move beyond a purely factual dependence, never a formational one.[143]

Regarding the cenobitical state, we have already seen that Romuald's first contact with cenobitical ambience when he was twenty was particularly disappointing. Later he would become gradually involved with the reform of cenobia but did not see the panaroma any more clearly. The disappointments often confused him during distressing times, as happened at Classe and Verghereto. A spirit like his could not remain indifferent when faced with the display of monastic customs far from the loftiness of monastic profession, but he advanced his difficult undertaking tirelessly and consistently. At Verghereto he even experienced the temptation to withdraw and close in on himself, so deeply embittered was he by the opposition and obstinacy of those monks. It was only by the Lord's grace that he succeeded in overcoming this crisis. 'When he was thrown out in such manner, he went off alone and a heavy sadness enveloped the depths of his soul, he considered completely abandoning the care of others' salvation and being satisfied . . . with only his own salvation . . . But such a fear then descended upon him that he was certain he would die and be condemned by divine judgment, should he persist in what he had been deliberating in his heart.'[144]

The necessary condition for the resumption of monastic life was a return to fidelity to the Rule which must maintain its indispensable role as guide and ideal. In this way the fervor of weary souls could be rekindled; the removal of unworthy abbots could be urged and, if necessary, imposed; and a simpler and poorer lifestyle could be re-established.

He undertook this assignment in faithfulness to the Rule each time the monks invested him with abbatial authority: 'He governed the monks under the strict discipline of the Rule, nor was anyone allowed to be absent without being punished... Mind's eye fixed on heaven, the holy man was not afraid to displease men while obeying God.'[145]

The criteria for order which Romuald adopted in his reform, were not identical everywhere. He chose freely between the options presented him as the situation demanded. At times he saw the cenobium working well next to the hermitage; at other times, quite separately. When both were viable, he preferred that there be one superior, possibly a resident hermit. He saw the difference in the two environments as complementary, though with characteristics and purposes specific to each. The ordinary routine entrusted the monastery with the task of caring for cenobitical formation and of preparing, when possible, candidates for the hermitage. 'Ordinary routine,' was flexible enough: it is clear that the holy reformer could never require cenobitical training as a requirement for acceptance into the hermitage. He wanted himself and the others to be free, in full awareness that each charism is a unique gift of the Holy Spirit (I Cor. 12.11).

The man of God always paid attention to the gifts the Spirit gave with sovereign freedom to each soul. Thus he became aware of the variety of expression for the religious life. He would support growth at each stage, and rooted himself in the conviction that no human institution could subsume the Spirit's actions. On the strength of this conviction, neither life in the cenobium nor in the hermitage represented for Romuald the apex of the ascetical journey. Both were to be seen in relation to further spiritual experiences, considered as logical consequences or natural outlets for one or the other. This is a question about the distinction between reclusion and evangelization, or in contemporary jargon, the nature of the apostolate.

Reclusion is a kind of ascetical life 'in which the freedom to give oneself to the Lord and enjoy contemplation's delights and embraces is really absolute.'[146] The monk or hermit-recluse who 'more closely imitating the anchoritism of the Desert Fathers, encloses himself in the small space of a cell, represents one of the loftiest developments of the monastic ideal. The brethren find in him the model of a life hidden with Christ in God.'[147] The same Saint Romuald remembered by historians as the founder of, or at least the one who re-evaluated reclusion in the Latin Church, lived as a recluse for several periods himself, the longest was the seven years at Sitria, as we have already seen.

Along with evangelization, reclusion is considered one of the eminent summits and values of the Romualdian-Camaldolese ideal. Beginning with the *Constitutions* of Blessed Rudolf in 1085, Camaldolese legislation has always been interested in safeguarding and using the institution of reclusion.[148] The *Camaldolese Constitutions* now in effect, approved by the Apostolic See in 1985, reaffirm the importance of this kind of life, leaving the possibility open and underlining the meaning of this Christian witness. It necessarily demands a lengthy experience of monastic life and the existence of indispensable 'psychological and ascetical components...a firm moral balance, reliable common sense, proven virtue.'[149]

The problem of defending the institution of reclusion against degeneration emerges simultaneously with the resolve to maintain it as a typical component of the Romualdian reform. Its charismatic character should be strongly indicated but never forced. The readiness to maintain reclusion under the fatherly care of the Prior endures, so the recluse is never considered exempt from the bonds of obedience. And the community of which the recluse is a member has its own role of encouragement and support, in harmony with their Prior. The hermitage of Camaldoli has a beautiful tradition of hermit-recluses who, from the beginning down to recent times, have left a significant, uncommon example of faith, living the apostolic values of prayer and voluntary expiation.

Some precise definitions already given for Romuald's life present the image of a free man, trained in the wisdom of the heart, keenly attentive to every impulse of the Spirit, and very sensitive to the Church's needs in his own day. So, he finds himself ready to open up to his disciples the mission road into pagan lands. Here, once again, is a text from the *Life of the Five Brothers* which is particularly indicative of the gradual nature and complementarity of the various states of ascetical life in the Romualdian-Camaldolese ideal.[150] The text states:

> The glorious Caesar (Otto III) conceived the project of sending some of the more fervent brothers of the hermitage to Poland. There they would construct a monastery in Christian territory, but near a pagan area, in beautiful woods offering a good retreat. And this would offer a threefold advantage to those seeking the Lord's way: the desired cenobium for novices coming from the world; the golden solitude of the hermitage for the mature monks thirsting for the living God; preaching the Gospel among the pagans for those who yearn to be free and live with Christ.[151]

In making the emperor's proposal his own, Romuald perceived therein that well-articulated multiplicity of choices and zeal which had greatly enriched his reforming activities. Without indulging in apologetics, we return to the text to grasp the theological meaning and significance of witness. The particular viewpoint of the Romualdian vision is located constantly by students of Camaldolese matters in the cenobium-hermitage marriage (connubio), but open to the possibility for an apostolic commitment which could also end up in martyrdom. We must add that encountering martyrdom, the summit of Christian witness, involved for the man of God and his disciples the fascinating and enticing idea that it ensured adequate space for the spiritual increase of souls in search of God, obedient to the Spirit's promptings.

In conclusion, it should be said that the apostolate and reclusion are seen as the two culminations of an upward journey whose stages are articulated in the threefold advantage (triplex bonum).[152] Beyond the impression of a certain schematizing which could be harmful to freedom of movement or when passing from one stage to another, Romuald's proposal can be even today a sign of presence alive and working in the human and Christian fabric.

Having pushed beyond the merely personal data—the indications of Romuald's personality and work—we are faced with a man of uncommon moral stature: an intelligent person guided by a clear and objective vision about the reality of the monastic and ecclesiastical world of his century. He was a courageous and balanced man, intentionally free in his movements, initiatives and decisions. A man rich in faith! Fused together, gifts of nature and grace have fashioned a master, father, reformer, founder, advisor, prophet, 'An ambassador between God and humanity who came to teach us the breadth of the Christian mystery and the urgent need to make life really Christian.'[153] Such a variety of ways of being and acting in his lifestyle and relationships brings Romuald close to us, though he lived a thousand years ago.

THE HERMITAGE AND MONASTERY OF CAMALDOLI
FROM THE FRONTISPIECE OF *CENNI STORICI*, FLORENCE 1864

two:

The Origins of Camaldoli

We have followed Romuald in the stages of his journey as reformer and itinerant monk, in the many complicated activities within the monastic and ecclesiastical worlds of his day. The founding of Camaldoli has not been on the route. The track followed is Peter Damian's, the first biographer, who does not accompany us to this place which is so important in the Camaldolese context: historically, culturally and spiritually.

The *Life of Romuald* makes no mention of Camaldoli and this, besides surprising us, gives rise to questions. The problem of Peter Damian's silence is not unsolvable because there is another equally reliable and authoritative source. In his study of Saint Peter Damian and his writings, Fr. Jean Leclercq has made this clarification about the *Life of Romuald:*

> Everything seems to support the premise that he (Peter Damian) was well informed. Yet he deliberately refrains from telling everything about his hero's life. 'I will not say everything, but everything I say will be true.'[154]

How do we explain Peter Damian's silence about the founding of Camaldoli? When Peter Damian wrote the *Life of Romuald,* Camaldoli was already twenty years in existence, having been founded by Romuald himself, as we shall see. The holy doctor knows Camaldoli, as can be seen in one of his letters which mentions a certain 'Martin, hermit of Camaldoli,'[155] who had informed him of an episode at the same place. Passing over the episode like that as he made reference, Peter Damian's mention of Camaldoli is very interesting, leading us to assume he really knew about the existence of Camaldoli.

The most common opinion among historians is that Peter Damian's silence about the foundation of the famous hermitage stems from the fact that in 1042, when the *Life* was being composed, Camaldoli did not yet merit attention. It was simply one among many of Romuald's eremitical foundations where probably nothing in particular had happened. Further, we know that Peter Damian did not give a complete listing of the Romualdian foundations. He himself tells us: 'The holy man lived in still many other locations...but we omit descriptions to avoid the tedium of an account which is too long.'[156]

So, the importance of Camaldoli is thought to have developed after the founder's time—and his biographer's as well. To know more, we must turn to the only existing historical source, reliable and wholly respectful of Peter Damian himself: Blessed Rudolf, the fourth prior of the Hermitage of Camaldoli.[157] Here is how this holy and scholarly man speaks to us in his *Rules for the Eremitical Life*, written in 1085, barely half a century after Saint Romuald's death:

> I, Rudolph, unworthy monk and priest, named Prior of the Hermitage of Camaldoli through the grace of Him who created me and not through any merits of my own... Realize, dearest brethren, that the above-mentioned Camaldolese hermitage was built by our holy Father-hermit Romuald through the Holy Spirit's inspiration and at the request of the Most Reverend Theodald, Bishop of Arezzo, along with a basilica which Bishop Theodald consecrated in honor of the Holy Savior in the year of the Incarnation, 1027. The saint built five cells and settled five religious brothers there: Peter, another Peter, Benedict, Gisso and Teuzo. He appointed one of them, Peter Dagnino, a prudent and holy man, as superior over the other four and told them to keep the rule of fasting, maintaining silence, and staying in the cell.
>
> That accomplished, he found another place farther down called Fonte Bono and built a house there. He settled there

a monk and three conversi (lay brothers) to receive guests, give them hospitality and a charitable meal, so that the Hermitage could always remain more hidden and distanced from the world's noises... Then he ordered Peter, whom he had appointed Prior, to build near the hospice of Fonte Bono a church which, with God's help, Peter built with great reverence and had consecrated by the bishop of Arezzo mentioned earlier.

What else? After diligently exhorting them, Blessed Romuald finally embraced them tearfully and left for Valdicastro. He built a monastery in the valley there and rendered his spirit to God. Christ manifested many miracles through Romuald both during his lifetime and after his death, referred to in his biography written by Peter Damian, a Catholic man, bishop and cardinal of the Holy Roman Church... God, the giver of all good things, had endowed those five brethren and conversi with such humility, patience, fortitude and constancy that their fame spread far. Many men began to come to the Hermitage after hearing about their good name—men from distant lands as well as from nearby—to listen to their kind conversation. Some of those received the monastic habit from Prior Peter, both from the common people and the nobility, all inspired by the Holy Spirit. These endowed the Hermitage with their legacies and began to live a life of penitence.[58]

Rudolf's testimony is incontestably valid. The diligent rendering of the details and circumstances well compensates for Peter Damian's silence. Camaldoli is Romuald's foundation, maybe the last in chronological order, but certainly his foundation.

Two questions: How long did Romuald stay at Camaldoli? In what year was the Hermitage of Camaldoli founded? The first question can be answered by stating that the lack of certain dates does not allow us to get our bearings on any definite time. Resigning ourselves to conjecture, we can say two years at the most. By deduction, however, we can be more exact about the foundation date. Bl. Rudolf, our only source, has given us an outline of a few essential details placed together with the utmost simplicity: a rather small church and five poor cells, more huts than substantial buildings. During Romuald's lifetime, this hermitage would have had relative importance, but never would have been privileged with any title designating its pre-eminent role among the other foundations of the holy hermit. So, Camaldoli acquired its importance after its beginnings. In fact, about a century had to pass before Camaldoli would find itself the head of a congregation of monasteries and hermitages, part of the ancient Benedictine lineage. That happened in 1113 when Pope Paschal II issued the Bull *Nostris Quidem Temporibus,* uniting under Camaldoli all the monasteries and hermitages founded or reformed by Saint Romuald, along with others which had adopted the Romualdian reform.[159] From that moment, the Camaldolese Congregation of the Order of Saint Benedict came into existence.[160]

In what year was Camaldoli founded? The traditional date assigned to the Hermitage's foundation is 1012. This date is unsubstantiated by any documentation. Bl. Rudolf specifies 1027 for the consecration of the church, but does not give any indication about the foundation date. The year 1012 was accepted for at least four centuries, but from the sixteenth and seventeenth centuries onwards, the first challenges arose. A little later, there would be direct opposition voiced by some critics, *e.g.* Mabillon[161] and the Camaldolese Abbot Guido Grandi.[162] The Camaldolese chroniclers Mittarelli and Costadoni opted for the traditional date, but without conviction, perhaps fearing the resumption of polemics—which had been smoothed over but not settled—between the hermits of Camaldoli and the bishop of Arezzo who claimed for himself certain stipulations of patronage over the Hermitage.

How did the 1012 date emerge? In our own time, Giovanni Tabacco took up the problem again and treated it competently. These are mainly his conclusions:[163] the 1012 date arose from false testimony given by Raniero, the Camaldolese Prior of Saint Michael of Arezzo. He made it on November 26, 1216, in the presence of Papal delegates, with the precise, shrewd intention of safeguarding the rights of exemption for the Hermitage of Camaldoli against any juridical and patrimonial claims advanced by the bishop of Arezzo. Raniero maintained he remembered Prior Placid of Camaldoli had shown some monks, himself among them, a notary's document in the year 1182 (thirty-four years earlier!) This document was said to have stated that the place 'where the Camaldoli hermitage is' was given to Romuald by one Maldolo, and gave the year 1012 as the time of donation.

While according zealous Raniero all the extenuating circumstances of his attachment to Camaldoli, likely a bit exaggerated, there are reasons for doubting the good faith of this prior, to the extent that we are forced to consider his deposition before the papal representatives devoid of any historical basis. The reasons are linked to the existence of an original document[164] of the previously mentioned Bishop Theodald, dated 1027. The document speaks of the foundation of the Camaldolese Hermitage as contemporary to the said bishop who, still in the same year, consecrated the church of the Holy Savior in the place called Campo Malduli belonging to the bishop of Arezzo and given by Theodald himself to Saint Romuald and his hermit disciples.[165] Besides, we have already seen Bl. Rudolf's testimony some ten years later,[166] which coincides exactly on names and dates with what is stated in Theodald's document.

The weight of these two documents persuades us to abandon the 1012 date for Camaldoli's birth in favor of placing it within the years 1023-1024 when Theodald was certainly occupying the episcopal throne in Arezzo.

Much has also been written about one Maldolo, Count or simply owner—then donor—of the Campo by the same name. Even though it is true that Maldolo is mentioned in the longer *Constitutions of Blessed Rudolf* in 1080,[167] historians now consider the figure of Maldolo imaginary and connected with 'a tradition later than Rudolf, evidently born out of a spontaneous legendary embellishment of the story about the origins.'[168] And if Maldolo appears alien to the documents of the period, he is no more than a legendary figure. In the best hypothesis, Maldolo could be the name of a certain owner, but one about whom nothing is historically certain.[169]

three:

The Camaldolese Congregation

The term *Camaldolese* has already surfaced several times. The meaning should have seemed more than obvious, even though the use of this adjective has, for various reasons, been incorrect. The term Camaldolese assumes its own specific significance only after St. Romuald's lifetime —in the year 1113, to be exact. Surely St. Romuald did not know the term, nor would his disciples for over a century of the Romualdian reform. In fact, we should use 'Romualdians' when referring to the people of these early times who followed the holy reformer and his accomplishments.

It is also true that some of the Holy Hermit's foundations and reforms would have been ephemeral, dying out after only a brief time and, sometimes, while St. Romuald was still alive. But his ideal and experience would survive his own death, as in the case of Camaldoli.

Camaldoli is a unique case which emerges and draws our attention to various matters and events of interest. From its humblest beginnings when it lacked even the least renown— Peter Damian ignored it—as one of the last, if not *the* last, of the Romualdian foundations, Camaldoli comes to recognition after a few decades of existence as though it is a focal point for other foundations. Clearly we are looking at the first development of a congregational aspect, fostered by the fame which now accompanies Prior Bl. Rudolf IV's *Rules for the Eremitical Life.*

During the priorship of Guido I, the sixth successor to St. Romuald, the Hermitage of Camaldoli already found itself the head of more than twenty monasteries and hermitages with a fair number of hermits, cenobites, nuns and oblates. Pope Paschal II issued the Bull *Nostris Quidem Temporibus* from Anagni on November 4, 1113,170 during the tenure of Guido I. The Bull juridically constituted the Camaldolese Congregation of the Order of Saint Benedict, deriving the name from Camaldoli which assumed the role of 'head and mother' of its own dependencies, as well as the hermitages and monasteries founded or reformed by St. Romuald, and those which had adopted the reform directives during the ensuing years.

Recognizing the Bull's importance, we note its most salient passages:

> To my venerable son Guido, Prior of Camaldoli, and to his legitimate successors in perpetuity.
>
> In our day, the religious importance of the Hermitage and Monastery of Camaldoli has spread and grown so much that, with God's grace, many monasteries have united into one congregation and many houses have adopted the same discipline, lifestyle and government, as though they were of one heart and soul.
>
> Hoping to preserve such unity in the Lord, we establish and ratify with this decree's authority, that no one of any order or dignity—clerical, monastic or lay—now or in the future, may lawfully remove in any way from this union and obedience those monasteries and houses which have accepted the discipline and lifestyle of the Hermitage and Monastery of Camaldoli and are now subject to its jurisdiction. We deem it useful, therefore, to list the individual names of these monasteries and houses in order to preserve their union.

This is the listing in the pontifical document:

> Six monasteries and one hermitage in the diocese of Arezzo; one monastery in the area of Bagno di Romagna; one hermitage in the region of Galeata; two monasteries in the Bologna diocese; two monasteries (one of which is for nuns) in the diocese of Florence; one monastery in the Fiesole diocese; five monasteries in the diocese of Volterra; four

monasteries in the Pisan diocese; two monasteries in the diocese of Lucca; two monasteries in the Sardinian diocese of Sassari; one hermitage in the Chiusi diocese: twenty-seven monasteries and three hermitages in all.

And so, we establish and confirm with the authority of this Apostolic See that these monasteries and all their property unite in perpetuity into one body under one head, namely the Prior of the Hermitage of Camaldoli, remaining subject to its monastic observances and under obedience to that prior who, with God's help, will be elected regularly by the abbots, priors and hermits.

We desire further to establish that this congregation remains forever under the protection of this Apostolic See, so that no bishop has the faculty to impose or retract excommunication from any of these monasteries without the Prior's consent and the Apostolic See's approval. The brethren have the faculty to receive the sacrament of Orders from any Catholic bishop they choose. We think it advisable to add that absolutely no one should cause anxiety for these monasteries, or take any of their possessions, or keep whatever has been taken from them, or reduce them to ruin with unjust quarrels, but all their property will be left intact for their support, administration and the benefit of all their needs.

And so, if any ecclesiastical or secular person in the future would knowingly try to transgress what we have here established, and would not have repaid with full satisfaction after being admonished a second and a third time, let that person be deprived of their rank of power and honor, held culpable for the sin committed before divine justice, be deprived of communion with the most holy body and blood of our God and Lord, Jesus Christ, and be subjected to a deserved punishment on the last day. But may the peace of our Lord Jesus Christ be with those who would be involved with these monasteries in a just manner, and so harvest here on earth the fruit of their good works and receive the reward of eternal life from the highest justice. Amen. Amen. Amen.

I, Paschal, bishop of the Catholic Church. Given at Anagni on November fourth in the year of the Lord 1113, the fifteenth of our pontificate.

At the point when Camaldoli found itself the head of an official congregation, it had already regulated itself with its own norms and customs which, as we have seen, Bl. Rudolf had collected in his *Constitutions* at the end of 1080. He speaks of a 'Prior'[171] elected by all the brethren of the Hermitage, by some of Fonte Bono and others of the 'congregation.' So, a regime existed in which one was declared responsible for supervision by an electoral body which would later be called 'Chapter.' Almost immediately, that responsible person would be given the title 'Prior General' and would not always be the actual prior of the Hermitage. With the *Constitutions of Gerard II* (+1290) around 1271, the figure of the Elder Father appeared, responsible for the exclusive governing of the Hermitage and Monastery of Camaldoli, while in the same period they always had two Visitators who had the duty of performing the canonical visitation of all the Camaldolese communities.

In 1183 we hear of a *sigillum* (seal) proper to Camaldoli, and consequently, to the entire congregation. The chroniclers who mention it state there is a more ancient document which mentions a 'Camaldolese coat-of-arms.' They give this description of it: two doves rampant drinking from a chalice around which is written the phrase: *Sigillum Sancti Salvatoris Camalduli.*'[172]

We have this heraldic description: 'Blue field; white doves with red legs and beaks; star rising above with a tail of fire; golden chalice with bright blood sipped by the two doves.'[173] An ancient tradition is referred to by Abbot Guido Grandi in his *Dissertationes*:[174] the union of the hermitage and the cenobium is the two doves, the contemplative and active dimensions of the monk who draws spiritual nourishment from the mystery of Christ symbolized by the chalice brimming with wine beneath the guidance of faith, symbolized by the star. The motto *Ego Vobis Vos Mihi* underlines the total and reciprocal belonging between the monk and God, and resounds an echo faithful to the great affirmation with which God strengthens the covenant with humanity: *I will be their God and they will be my people* (Ez. 37.27).'

four:

Historical Figures

Thusfar, we have accompanied the Camaldolese Congregation at its birth and as it places itself institutionally into history. But it is very important to take a parallel path through its various charismatic projections, presented in the people whose charisms are representative: the saints first of all, but also the various scholars and artists.

What is most striking is the wonderful variety of ways with which the same Spirit who is manifold in gifts and manifestations,[175] has acted in the diverse but convergent lives of these persons who are all involved in the one aim of monastic life: seeking God. And so, we have the hermit and the recluse; the monk and the penitent; the hidden pearl of the humble one and the light placed on the candle stand of pastoral ministry; the wisdom of the unlearned and the knowledge of the scholar; the anonymous worker and the one who has left notable contributions in the world of art.

Variety in people and in the choice of adopted paths is encouraged in the Camaldolese tradition. It has always guaranteed within the one monastic ambit marked diversity in environments and circumstances. The multiform experience lived by Saint Romuald in obedience to the Spirit 'who lived in his heart,'[176] has been a model for the ascetical journey of his followers.

We have recognized in Master Romuald an extremely liberated man, but one who never shirked the commitments assumed when he professed himself a monk; a man firmly anchored in the tradition without allowing himself to be carried away by any kind of formalism; a man novel in his intuitions and solutions, but never vain or ambitious.

And so are his disciples: at Camaldoli, Fonte Avellana, Pereo, Sitria, Cuxa and Valdicastro—wherever Providence wants these witnesses of the Kingdom. When holiness is real, it flees programs and systems because the Spirit is above every kind of pressure. Human existence and the greatest affirmation of humanity, holiness, rely on supreme values which no one and nothing can compromise. Monasticism must be always watchful and prepared to eliminate every compromise, so as not to risk becoming a withered branch on a living tree, the Church.

The scope of these remarks does not permit a complete listing of these people who, docile to the Spirit, 'as inexperienced ones, have learned prudence; the foolish have become wise.'[177] Here are gathered some of the more expressive figures, those who can give us a good picture of the Camaldolese ideal. Logically, we begin with some of the immediate disciples of Saint Romuald who, formed in his school, shared the grace of fraternal communion with him and are the most precious legacy of his spiritual fatherhood. Since we already spoke about some of them as circumstances demanded, we limit ourselves simply to reporting their names in chronological order with brief, specific details. But we furnish facts and fuller details about others to fill out their personality and type of witness.

St. Peter Orseolo +982

Peter was Doge of Venice when he decided to follow Saint Romuald, renouncing his reign after two years of governing. Along with Marino, the coarse first master of Romuald, and Saint John Gradenigo, he followed the saint of Ravenna to Cuxa at the foot of the Pyrenees where he lived as a hermit until he died on January 11, 982.[178]

SS.. Benedict, John, Matthew, Isaac and Christian +1003

These are the 'Five Brothers' whose *Life* was written by Saint Bruno Boniface. The first two were disciples of Saint Romuald at the Hermitage of Pereo and missionaries to Poland; the other three were Polish men who had joined the latter in their work of evangelization. All five were martyred near Casimiria on November 11, 1003.[179]

St. Bruno of Querfurt (Bruno Boniface) +1009

Bruno is the disciple who best assimilated the Holy Reformer's teaching and experience, and became Saint Romuald's favorite disciple. He is the author of the *Life of the Five Brothers,* the first basic Romualdian-Camaldolese document. He was consecrated archbishop *ad gentes* (for the nations) and preached the Gospel in the western regions of Russia in the Kingdom of Kiev where he was martyred on February 9, 1009.[180]

Bls. Peter Dagnino +1051
Peter, Benedict, Gisso and Teuzo, +11th c.

These are the first five hermits Saint Romuald wanted with himself at the foundation of the Hermitage of Camaldoli. Excelling in virtues and austerity, they proved themselves worthy to begin this distinguished foundation which became within barely a century's passing the head of the Camaldolese Congregation. Peter Dagnino was particularly esteemed by Saint Romuald who designated him as his first successor in guiding the small eremitical band.[181]

Guido, Monaco, or Guido of Arezzo +1058

We cannot document with the certainty of some historians that Guido really was Romualdian or Camaldolese. We know he was a native of Arezzo, and that he made monastic profession at Pomposa under Abbot Saint Guido, and probably spent a later period of eremitical life at both Camaldoli and Fonte Avellana.

Guido distinguished himself through his love of music, the field in which he revealed his true genius. Entrusted with teaching chant to the young monks at his abbey, he dedicated himself to finding a simpler method for reading and learning music to substitute for the very complicated method then in use. In Guido's day, in fact, reading and singing music was arduous, and only a few were able to sing without mistakes: 'they sing the greater part by ear, *per usum,*'[182] with the consequence of inexact performances passed down from person to person, from choir to choir. Before Guido, the neumes were placed on an open field and their notation determined practically if the volume should be high, low or in the middle. Guido's reform enlarged the scale of sounds from four (tetrachord) to six (hexachord), giving a name to each sound in such a way that interpreting and the special reading of each note from its respective shape was now eliminated. There would be only seven successive sounds, octave after octave.

Guido drew the names for the musical notes from the first syllable of each hemistich of the first strophe from the First Vespers' hymn of the feast of Saint John the Baptist, which already had the sounds for climbing the scale:

UT queant laxis   REsonare fibris
MIra gestorum   FAmuli tuorum
SOLve polluti   LAbii reatum Sancte Johannes

With these six syllables (UT, RE, MI, FA, SOL, LA) Guido singled out and named the corresponding notes with the great advantage of now being able to follow them and sing them in their exact intonation. Such a process suggested the basic rule to Guido, that all the notes placed on the same line must be executed with the same tone. So, the transcription was no longer written on an open field, but on a staff of four lines and three spaces.

He also became famous for writing *Micrologus,* a didactic work of great value which, besides offering norms about the modulation of the various tones, facilitated the reading of old musical codices. And he compiled an

Antiphonary which was adopted in many monasteries, cathedrals and schools throughout Europe. He is also known for his letter to a monk named Michael about an obscure melody *(de ignoto cantu)*. Guido lucidly explained the principles and rules for a more immediate and faithful execution of chant, and is considered quite rightly the inventor of today's system of musical notation.[183]

But despite the general acclaim with which the Guidonian musical reform was welcomed, his own monastic confreres at Pomposa assembled a host of objections. Perhaps they had an aversion to innovation (often the case with monks), or perhaps they were envious, given Guido's many admirers continually requesting his works. Whatever the cause, Guido was rather annoyed and felt compelled to leave his own monastery, with his abbot's approval.[184]

Where did he go? Certainly many bishops wanted him as the music instructor in their cathedral chapels. He also went to Rome, summoned by Pope John XX (r. 1024-1033) for the same reason. In his letter to the monk Michael, Guido himself refers to the admiration shown him by the pontiff. Besides these moves in connection with teaching his musical method, some historians[185] believe that Guido lived at Fonte Avellana for a period of eremitical life and maybe, at Camaldoli, where he would have known Saint Romuald. But as enticing as these suggestions may be, they are only hypotheses. Guido would have been in contact with Saint Peter Damian at Fonte Avellana, having known him at Pomposa when the holy doctor was summoned there—we are certain of this—by Abbot Saint Guido to instruct his monks. Guido's return to Pomposa is surely due to the kind persistence of the aforementioned holy abbot. He lived his last years there, from 1050 to 1058.

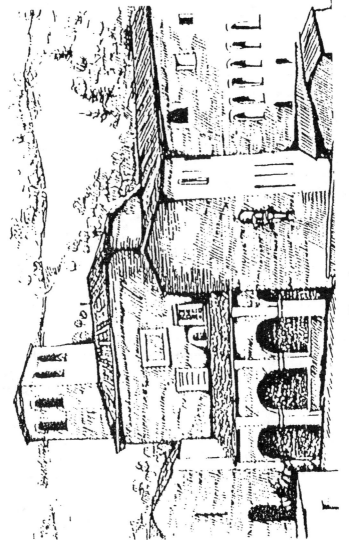

Fonte Avellana

St. Peter Damian +1072

Peter was born at Ravenna of a well-to-do family. But while still a baby, his father died and his mother, who was already burdened with too many children, rejected him. Rescued by a neighbor, he was later adopted by one of his older brothers named Damian. He was fond of the child, raised him and made him study. Grateful, Peter added his brother's name to his own. When he was of age, he passed to higher studies at Ravenna, then at Faenza and Parma where he studied philosophy and rhetoric to his great benefit.

In 1034, he had occasion to meet and speak with two monks of Fonte Avellana on their way to Parma. He was attracted to their sanctity and modesty, and later followed them to their hermitage, becoming a monk there. Peter lived almost his entire life at Fonte Avellana, with the exception of intervals, some brief, others prolonged by important obligations entrusted to him by the popes of his day, as we shall see.

He immersed himself in the monastic and ascetical life with great ardor, helped and stimulated by the examples of the venerable hermits. In short, 'loins girded with faith and the practice of works ... under the Gospel guidance' he became a diligent pupil and skilled in the 'school of the Lord's service.'[186] He dedicated himself to almost constant prayer which he prolonged at Vigils; to the austerity of the common life at the hermitage regarding fasting; to penance and silence. Simultaneously he followed a course of study with amazing diligence and began to write those works which would fashion him a master 'of the spiritual arts.'

As proof of his remarkable progress, the holy abbot Guido of Pomposa requested his presence for a prolonged instruction of his monks, only five years after his entrance into Fonte Avellana; Peter spent two years at Pomposa. In 1042 he was at St. Vincent at Furlo in the Fossombrone diocese where he wrote the *Life of Romuald,* gathering notes from the direct disciples of the Holy Hermit and Reformer, thus becoming his first biographer.

In 1043 he was elected prior of Fonte Avellana. He poured his heart and experience into this service, becoming a true father of souls. The band of Avellaniti hermits grew and the holy prior provided more breathing–space for his community by founding the Hermitage of Montepregio near Perugia in 1053. In 1054 he founded the Hermitage of Camporeggiano near Gubbio. He also enlarged his own Hermitage of Fonte Avellana, furnishing a small cloister near the church, as well as other buildings, many of which still stand today. He provided the hermitage with a good library, without neglecting to enrich the church as much as possible with new furnishings for the liturgical celebrations.

But the best of his learned and illumined mind has come to us in the vast output of his writings which point out his more urgent worries, particularly on the moral and spiritual orders. In 1057 he wrote a *Rule for the Eremitical Life* for his brethren which explains the ascetical/theological principles of monastic *conversatio*, including the necessary applications of an organized and disciplined nature. For all practical purposes, he was the real initiator of the Avellanita Congregation which Pope Pius V incorporated into the Camaldolese Congregation in 1569.

In 1057 he was also chosen bishop of Ostia and created a cardinal by Pope Stephen IX. From now on, Peter Damian would find himself more involved, in spite of himself, in the most serious problems of the Church in his day: simony; a corrupt clergy; the base sale of bishoprics and abbacies to the highest bidder, with the inevitable moral decadence of licentious living—gluttony, revelry and brazen concubinage. And it was, of course, the people of God who suffered the effects, being more uneducated, abandoned and torn by the many scandals. Feeling himself a monk and hermit to the core, Peter Damian never meant to escape the Church's urgent needs. He always saw the Church as being in need of more help, more prophetic voices and authentic people who would spend themselves in a serious, immediate reform on all levels. Some of his writings, particularly certain letters, clearly demonstrate the torments of his spiritual combat between a twofold and contrasting love for the solitude of the cloister and the kindled word; searching for God and the duty of not abandoning the brethren. Withdrawing and thinking only to himself how it would be easier (though he always felt repugnance for what was 'easier') to stay strongly rooted in his lifestyle at his beloved hermitage where, among other things, a band of brethren reclaimed the presence and teaching of their father. One supposes he recalled what he had written about Saint Romuald: 'not staying enclosed in hidden solitude, but going further where he could acquire more souls; not burning like a coal for himself alone, but as a lamp on the lampstand to spread the rays of his light to all those in God's house.'[187]

Zeal for the Lord's house agreed with his own combative spirit and the desire to restore Christ's Spouse to her beauty, thrust him there where he revealed himself greatly changed: 'the reformer sprang from the monk.'[188] First of all, he understood that the journey of a true reform is born from within the Church, so he began with himself and his monks, convinced that it would be useless to thunder out words without following them up with the force of life's witness. Demanding and uncompromising in the face of vices, he was no less demanding of himself. The austerity of life which he proposed to revive among the clergy and laity, he always demonstrated in his own lifestyle and actualized within himself. This monk, bishop and cardinal shouted out with his life and the force of his virtue, before using the burning eloquence of rhetoric.

The first occasion which placed Peter Damian in the forefront of ecclesiastical events of his day was the schism provoked by Benedict X (+1059), the antipope who had been installed at the Lateran after Stephen IX died in 1058. Peter had known and maintained bonds of friendship with the monk Hildebrand, the future Pope Gregory VII (+1073) and, in full agreement with him, did all he could to bring about the election of a new legitimate Pontiff in the person of Nicholas II.

After straightening out the schism, Pope Nicholas II sent Peter Damian as his legate to Milan where the people and lower clergy had rebelled against their simoniacal archbishop. He calmed and resolved that controversy, as another schism headed by Bishop Cadalus of Parma burst onto the scene. He too was simoniacal and again, Peter Damian trimmed the sails of revolt by bringing about the legitimate election of Pope Alexander II in 1061. Not much later, he was sent to Cluny to resolve an old controversy between the monks and their local bishop. He returned to Italy and had to rush to Florence for a situation analogous to Milan's. He also brought this legation to a successful conclusion. When Germany was in tumult over the attempted divorce of Bertha of Savoy by Henry IV, Peter Damian convoked and presided over the Council of Magonza, succeeding in subduing the emperor.

He was finally able to return to Italy and concentrated on Fonte Avellana, but only for a while. A new legation entrusted to him by the Pope took him to Ravenna, his homeland, to straighten out the various controversies there. 'Seven legations, one after the other, all brought safely to port with his personal charm and his invincible strength of character.'[189]

Historians and the majority of people who have written about Peter Damian are full of admiration and praise for this man who, along with the monk Hildebrand, was considered a pillar of the Church in his day. But there is no better judge of him than Pope Alexander II who said when presenting him to the French bishops as his legate to the synod of Chalon: 'Because we are so busy with many Church affairs, we ourselves are unable to attend, so we are sending a man who has the greatest authority in the Church other than ourself. This is Peter Damian, bishop of Ostia; he is our eye and the firm foundation of the Apostolic See.'[190]

If Peter Damian's presence and work show him decisive in sorting out disputes and re–establishing communion where it had been shattered, his writings ended up being just as decisive and efficacious. Peter Damian left behind many works of theological polemics, works which won him the title 'Doctor of the Church' which was bestowed on him by Pope Leo XII in 1872. Here is a simple summary of his writings:

• One hundred and fifty-seven letters to popes, Cadalus the antipope, cardinals, patriarchs, archbishops and bishops, priests, deacons, clerics, abbots and monks, leaders, famous people and private individuals: divided into eight books;

• Seventy-seven sermons and homilies on Christ's Mysteries, the Blessed Virgin Mary and the Saints, spread throughout the twelve months of the liturgical calendar;

• Four lives of saints;

• Sixteen books or booklets about various theological topics;

• Some prayers, liturgical hymns and poetry.

Peter Damian's style is polished and elegant, often characterized by frank openness, sometimes polemical. It also carries a touching delicacy, approaching tenderness, particularly in his prayers and hymns. His Latin makes for nimble and lively sentences, echoing rhetorical timbre. One reads him with pleasure and attention.

None of his contemporaries was his theological equal. Although dogmas and faith-affirmations are not treated in a systematic manner with an overall vision, he still succeeds in treating in a thorough and scholarly fashion those truths most discussed and debated in his own day. 'He writes on the Trinity against the final diatribes of heretics from the first centuries of Church history; he writes about divine omnipotence, against the early medieval philosophers who abused Aristotelian philosophy; he writes about the Messiah, (against the Jews) and on the procession of the Holy Spirit (against the Greeks). He does not properly distinguish speculative theology from practical theology. He unites them and, depending on his needs, usually treats one or the other... His theology is positive and incredibly biblical. He knows the canons perfectly, cites the councils, and often the Fathers. He has taken much of his style from Saints Gregory and Leo. But the field where his erudition...has no limits is Holy Scripture.'[191]

Some saintly disciples were formed in his school. Among them we note: Saint Dominic Loricato (+1060) who was extraordinary in penitential asceticism; Saint John of Lodi (+1105), his secretary and diligent copyist of his writings who was with him on some of his legations, wrote the Life of Peter Damian and who was chosen bishop of Gubbio; and Blessed Leo, hermit-recluse of Fonte Avellana to whom Peter Damian turned for counsel and teaching.

On the return trip from his final legation at Ravenna, Peter Damian became sick. He died while staying at the monastery of Holy Mary in Faenza on February 22, 1072. In his *Paradiso*, Canto twenty-one of *The Divine Comedy*, Dante Alighieri (+1221) has marked out a profile of Peter Damian which is among the truest and most complete. This profile is more moral than physical. The great articulations of Camaldolese life: cenobium, hermitage, evangelization; and specific marks corresponding to monastic formation: ascetical formation, contemplation and the apostolate, come from the mouth of the holy doctor. They are aptly put by this greatest of poets who, many believe, thoroughly knew Peter Damian's writings.

We also possess an epigraph of our saint. He himself spoke it for his tomb. While reflecting his austere and honest spirit, it emerges as a document of Christian witness which engenders in people of all eras serious thoughts inviting us to fix our gaze beyond the empiricals of earthly life:

> What you are, I once was; what I am, you will be.
> Do not put your faith in perishable things.
> Dreams are vanities which precede reality;
> The eternal centuries follow the brief years.
> Live mindful of death that you may live forever.
> What you see passes; what remains is very near.
> Oh how well he provided, the one who left you, perverse world,
> Who died first to flesh with his body
> That he not die to the world with his flesh!
> He preferred heavenly to earthly things, eternal to fleeting things.
> Now free, you return the soul to its source;

The spirit ascends on high, goes back to its source,
Disregarding what is beneath itself, everything which pulls
    it down.
Remember me, I beg you; watch these ashes of Peter;
Pray, weep and say: *Lord, pardon him.*[192]

Bl. Rudolf, fourth Prior of the Hermitage of Camaldoli +1088

Rudolf was among the most eminent figures at the Camaldoli Hermitage, noted for his sanctity and doctrine. We do not have any record of his life until he appears as Prior of Camaldoli in 1074. His predecessors had been Peter Dagnino, disciple of Saint Romuald, Albizo and Rustico. We can consider Rudolf as Camaldoli's first author of historical importance and the wise organizer of the monastic eremitical life at Camaldoli which would become the head and mother of a Congregation within a few years. This became possible chiefly through the boost given by the important *Constitutiones Camaldulenses* or *Liber Vitae Eremiticae* written by Rudolf in two different drafts: the longer draft in 1080 and the shorter version in 1085.

Through his contribution of this legislation, Camaldoli came to be in the position of a pilot, so to speak, imparting to the future Congregation its own nature and its own role in the Church. Historians give Blessed Rudolf the title *Doctor Eximius* (exceptional doctor), surely for this reason. He enlarged the hospice of Fonte Bono and fashioned it a monastery capable of sustaining many monks. Between 1085 and 1086 he founded the first women's monastery at Luco di Mugello near Florence, which he made subject to his own hermitage, uniting other monasteries and churches there later on. He died in 1088.

The *Constitutiones Camaldulenses* are firstly a wise and precise theological exposition of eremiticism, rooted in Sacred Scripture and the classical tradition of the Fathers, and secondarily a normative and disciplinary tract. After confirming the superiority of eremitical life which obviously presupposes a real experience of mystical contemplation, allowing the hermit to savor the joys of habitual communion with God, Rudolf affirms and requires a lengthy previous maturation period in cenobitical life. He bases his own assertion on experience which convinced him that a different procedure ordinarily causes failures and difficulties.

Camaldoli's legislator wanted to protect the life of the Hermitage with some observances which would foster contemplation: *lex jeiunandi atque silendi et in cellis permanendi* (law for fasting, keeping silence and staying in the cell). Fasting, silence and stability are advised not as an end in themselves but as essential means for attaining real interior purification and creating the spiritual and material environment which most favors contemplation.

In order to invest the hermit life with such a possibility, the hermit must not be a novice-beginner, but an experienced monk who has already arrived at certain levels of faith's journey which permit him to move with full freedom without letting him consider himself dispensed from listening to the Holy Spirit's voice. Supposing such a maturity, the Prior should act more as a brother than as a superior to the hermit and should choose his advisors from among the hermits for the good management of his service. The Prior does not prevent access to higher expressions of evangelical witness such as reclusion and the apostolate for those hermits of proven virtue who, driven by the Spirit's voice, request such witness or even better, are those in whom the Prior himself discerns the capacity for such witness.

Rudolf states it is normal for hermits to be fewer than the cenobites, suitably so for that requirement of a qualitative superiority of ascetical living at the hermitage. Regarding observance, he proposes that monks faithfully draw only from the *Rule of St. Benedict*, always considered the classical norm for a serious cenobitical formation which can suitably prepare one for the eremitical life. But the passage from cenobium to hermitage should be supervised, allowed or advised only by the Prior who St. Benedict intended to be an expert in divine law, establishing or ordering nothing against the Lord's teaching, but dedicated to making it penetrate his orders and his own teaching like the yeast of perfection.[193] If on the one hand, Rudolf affirms that the duty of the eremitical life is common to all, at least in theory, allowing it in practice is subject to the Prior's judgment. And the Prior must not refuse it without serious reason. If a greater freedom is allowed the hermit, this is acceptable because it presupposes a long experience of clear and proven virtue, particularly obedience and humility, but primarily because the unquestioned primacy of the Holy Spirit acting within souls must be taken into account.

Rudolf does not presume to present his doctrine as simple fact, even if from his own personal experience. He supports it with many examples revealed by Sacred Scripture: Moses, David, Elijah, Elisha, Rachel, Leah, and particularly John the Baptist, Jesus, and the ancient Fathers like St. Benedict and St. Romuald, the latter who

> after placing himself under monastic discipline and having accepted pastoral ministry, finally passed on to the struggle of the hermitage and built many locations for the eremitical life, among which he built this Hermitage of Camaldoli in a wonderful way.[194]

As we see, the criterion Rudolf follows repeats the dictates of the classical tradition of the Fathers and it is this which ensures the perennial vitality of his doctrine. He writes a clear, incisive, flowing Latin which facilitates comprehension.

> Silence without meditation is dead, like the tomb of the living dead; meditation without silence reaches no conclusion...United in spiritual marriage, they are deep quiet of soul and peak of contemplation...To come to the hermitage is supreme perfection; not to live in the hermitage with perfection is supreme damnation.[195]

Three Bishop–Saints:
I. St. John of Lodi +1105

John was born at Lodi in 1040. As an intelligent and holy youth, he attentively kept control of his habits with integrity, guarding his innocent youth. He studied well and, careful with his spiritual progress, dedicated himself lovingly to charitable works for the needy. When he was twenty, he wanted to find a solitary corner not far from his area where he could take up the hermit life, but hearing about the hermits of Fonte Avellana a little later, he embarked on the long voyage and retreated there into solitude, welcomed by St. Peter Damian.

The holy prior's insight immediately grasped in this youth the real possibility for successful monastic *conversatio* and their two spirits joined in reciprocal emulation: one becoming the father; the other, the favored disciple. John had a delicate constitution, yet never dispensed himself from the Hermitage's rigorous observances. He organized and corrected his prior's writings. When Peter Damian was chosen cardinal-bishop, John frequently accompanied him on his apostolic legations. He was elected prior of Fonte Avellana upon the death of the saintly Doctor and Master.

Though he was very meek and reluctant to accept any dignity whatever, Saint John used the priorship as an opportunity to pour out his soul's riches upon his confreres and to show his own great love for the poor. A great famine plaguing the entire area forced a large throng of needy people to knock on the door of the Avellanita Hermitage. The prior gave freely as much as possible to alleviate their sufferings, confident that his confreres too, like himself, would take on greater and more rigid abstinence in order to provide adequate help to others. He even decided to sell the silver off the altar and went to Apulia to buy wheat to perform better the tasks of Christian charity.

He was named bishop of Gubbio against his will in 1103. He was there only two years, but his episcopate, though brief, was distinguished, just like his priorship, for eminent works of help and welfare for every needy individual. He died on September 7, 1105, at the age of sixty–five.

II. *St. Raniero, martyr +1179*

We know nothing about Raniero's birth. Around 1154, we find him a monk of Fonte Avellana where, that same year, he was called to hold the episcopal throne at Cagli, about ten kilometers from the Hermitage on the Flaminian road.[196] As bishop, he met the demands of pastoral service, in the middle of many controversies and sufferings for some twenty years, due mainly to the disobedient clergy whose excesses in lifestyle often left them overwhelmed by the care of property and possessions, much to their discredit among the good people. Bound by a close friendship with Saint Ubald, the holy and saintly bishop of Gubbio, Raniero went to him for advice and was wisely encouraged to persevere with resolute patience in guiding the diocese with the same style he had already begun.

But the problems turned into hostilities and they no longer counted on petitions to the Apostolic See. In 1175 Pope Alexander III (+1181) resolved the problem by naming Raniero Archbishop of Spalato and Primate of Dalmatia and Istria, which was still part of the Byzantine Empire at that time. When Alexander III went to visit the Emperor Barbarossa in 1177, the Dalmatian Primate accompanied him from Lissa to Zara and took part in the Lateran Council that same year with the suffragan bishops.

As at Cagli, his intrepid strength was again put to the test at Spalato, this time by some country gentlemen usurping the Church's rights. Raniero did not agree to the injustice, knowing that his position was becoming more precarious with each passing day.

Meanwhile, some Croatian princes had seized some ecclesiastical property. Raniero appealed to the Emperor in vain, and tried every way to effect a peaceful settlement. Refusing payment, the princes took to scorning the bishop and his duty to safeguard the Church's property which was meant to sustain those who were more needy. A critical situation arose which led the princes to cut things short and resort to arms and stones with which they ruthlessly murdered the holy bishop on August 11, 1179. Spalato venerates him as a martyr and as one of its patrons. Archdeacon Thomas of the twelfth century wrote his life and handed down to us the story of his martyrdom.

III. *Rinaldo +1225*

When he was twenty-five, Rinaldo decided to enter the monastic life and chose Fonte Avellana, where he had been studying during preceding years. He lived there for thirty-six years, seriously committed to real spiritual growth. In 1217, he was charged with the Prior Generalate of the Avellanita Congregation. The following year, he was chosen bishop of Nocera Umbra. Postignano in the area around Nocera Umbra, is the native land of the noble family of the Counts Trinci.

Episcopal dignity and pastoral duties did not prevent him from maintaining the tenor of his austere life. This permitted him the means with which to help the poor all the more. He welcomed a young orphan into the bishop's palace where he shared with him his daily frugal meal. He had asked him to sit at the head of the table, holding a knapsack over his shoulder, to remind the bishop and his priests of the poor and pilgrim Christ present in the orphan.

He was a close friend of *Il Poverello* of Assisi, Saint Francis, and Rinaldo may very well have been one of seven bishops present at the consecration of the Porziuncola and the proclamation of the famous indulgence. He died one year before Francis on February 9, 1225. He is the patron of Nocera Umbra.

Gratian, Monaco +1175

The fame of this monk is completely linked with his work, the *Concordantia Discordantium Canonum o Decretum,* which won him the epithet *Pater Canonici Juris* (Father of Canon Law).

We are not certain about the details of his birth. More than one city claims to have been his birthplace—Bologna,

GRATIAN, FATHER OF CANON LAW

Chiusi, Pisa, Orvieto and Civitavecchia—but none has documented proof to claim this longed-for honor. Another hypothesis which was assimilated by the *Annales Camaldulenses*[197] which, in turn, derives from the *Cronicon Clusinum* by Sigibert, would have Gratian the monk as bishop of Chiusi. However, it is difficult to move beyond opinion. We do know that Gratian was a monk of Saints Nabore and Felix in Bologna when he published his *Decretum* in 1150. That monastery had been under Camaldoli for about forty years and had become part of the Camaldolese Congregation. At Bologna, Gratian developed his business as 'Reader and Master of Law' keeping a desk in his own monastery. His name is synonymous with the work known as *Gratian's Decretum*.

The great importance and renown of his work lies in it being a comprehensive compilation of the canons and decrees issued by the popes and councils before his own time. Following, we suppose, the system already established by scholasticism, he obtained the scattered and disorganized materials from various known sources: the Bible (obviously), the *Canones Apostolorum,* the conciliar canons, papal decrees, works of the Fathers and ecclesiastical writers for both the universal Church and local churches. He entrusted to the history of law this organic work which has remained the surest document for juridical information, among the other documents which hold legal force.

As far as its structure is concerned, we quote from the *Enciclopedia Italiana*:

> Gratian's collection is divided into three parts. The first part includes one hundred and one *distinctiones,* subdivided into *canones or capita;* the first twenty distinctions (initium or principium) constitute an introduction to its general concepts and sources; the others (tractatus ordinandorum) concern ecclesiastical persons and offices. This division into parts is Gratian's; the subdivision into distinctiones is the work of Paucapalea, Gratian's disciple. The second part of the *Decretum* is divided into thirty *causae;* each causa is subdivided into *quaestiones* which are subdivided into

canones. Each causa represents a controversial case of law; the quaestiones are the various juridical problems stemming from it, and Gratian responds to these, offering his solution with the authority of the canones. This part contains the penal law and trial law, norms for ecclesiastical property, laws for religious and matrimonial law. Some groups of causae and each individual causa are indicated by a particular name: *tractatus decretalium, causa simoniacorum, tractatus coniugii,* etc. The third quaestiona of causa thirty-three speaks about penance and is named *de poenitentia;* it was not divided by Gratian, but by others, into seven distinctiones subdivided into canones. The third part of the *Decretum* is concerned with liturgical matters and is called de *consecratione or Liber de Sacramentis;* Paucapalea also repartitioned this section into five distinctiones and canones. The distinctions and questions of the causae were later divided into *partes* by Guido da Baiso.[198]

The great Dante grasped the significance of this Camaldolese monk's compiled work and fixes his portrait with a few, well chosen expressions, like brush-strokes of a master painter. The poet locates the monk Gratian in the fourth heaven, or Sun of Canto Ten of *Il Paradiso,* among the twelve wise spirits who are presented to Dante by St. Thomas Aquinas, on whose lips the poet places these words:

> *That other flame glows*
> *with Gratian's smile,*
> *who helped in one court or the other*
> *and is now pleased in Paradise*

> *(Par. X, 103–105)*

Four Hermit Recluses at Camaldoli: Bl. Pellegrine, Bl. Simon, Bl. Michael Pini, Ven. Louis Massei.

We witness these men following Christ at the Hermitage of Camaldoli. The first two were contemporaries at an earlier time than the others. All four lived out here their humble and silent fidelity, their joyous experience of communion with God, their commitment, and heroic asceticism.

Certain ideas have already emerged from preceding pages about reclusion, that typically Romualdian institution which the Camaldolese tradition has continued and guarded up to the present day, always recognizing in it, along with evangelization, the highest goal of the monastic eremitical journey. Camaldoli's legislation in particular, through the great Priors General Blessed Martin III (+1258), Blessed Gerard II (+1291) and Venerable Bonaventure (+1348), watched over and defended reclusion with devotion, always keeping alive their esteem and regard for this kind of life at the very bosom of the Congregation. This legislation, codified into proper constitutions, foresaw and consistently claimed a central role of the first order for the recluse, without excusing him from the obedience owed his prior.

The *Life of Camaldolese Hermits* and *Book IV On Customs* by the aforementioned Gerard, foretell that the Hermitage will never lack the penitentiary, normally the recluse who hears the confreres' confessions, and those of devotees who also turn to him. A resolute stability in the cell is asked of the one who makes profession as a recluse, but not the absolute silence of the other hermits because his word and presence are sought for domestic counsels, definitors at General Chapters, and as reformers in special visitations whenever the Prior General deems it necessary.[199] No norm exempts recluses from possibly being elected prior, or even Prior General, as in the case of Blessed James, a penitentiary who, after spending a good period in the Generalate, renounced it. Strongly attracted to solitude, he returned to reclusion to finish out his days during the thirteenth century.

These four holy recluses noted here represent the many, who experienced this venerable lifestyle.

I. *Bl. Pellegrine +1291*

Pellegrine is believed to have been a member of the Conti Guelfi family of Banzena in Casentino.[200] Before becoming a hermit recluse at the Sacred Hermitage of Camaldoli, he was abbot of the Holy Mary in Isola cenobium near Galeata.

We do not know how long he was abbot there, but we are sure that he renounced the abbacy for spiritual reasons, motivated by a great desire for solitude. Handing in his resignation to Prior General Gerard II in 1280, he came to the Camaldoli Hermitage where, for reasons known only to Gerard, it was easy for him to enter reclusion.

Now that he had reached his ideal, Pellegrine so committed himself and his progress there was so extraordinary that, within a few years, he was blessed with renowned mystical gifts by God. There are reports that in 1287 he had some visions which are still famous in Camaldoli's history. Some of the visions are recounted in the writings of Blessed Simon, who was also a recluse and Pellegrine's confessor. Love of music was a striking personal gift for him and he improved the chant. He put to music the hymns and other liturgical excerpts from the *Ordo Divinorum Officiorum,* composed by Prior General Martin III (+1258).

Despite the notable steps in this saintly hermit's journey of faith, we know that he lived a period of such total spiritual aridity that he was at the point of being tempted to leave the Hermitage and return to the world. Andrea Munoz asserts that Blessed Pellegrine withstood the test (which must have been most difficult) through a special divine intervention. He had his remarkable visions after this tormented period of his life. The entire text of these visions has not come down to us; we only know a fragment which was recovered from beneath Pellegrine's head in 1693 when his bones were moved to a new grave, now within the Pope's Chapel at the Camaldoli Hermitage.

He was the Elder Father of the Hermitage for some time, thereby functioning as the Prior General's Vicar. When the General passed to a better life in 1291, Blessed Pellegrine had to convene the General Chapter for the election of Gerard's successor. A little later in that same year, the blessed recluse also passed to the joys of the Heavenly Jerusalem.

II. *Bl. Simon +1292*

Simon was Blessed Pellegrine's spiritual director. Born in Genoa, he seems to have become a hermit of Camaldoli at a fairly young age. A few years later, he requested and received reclusion, and remained a recluse until his death. Gifted with a lively intelligence and good education, he spent much of his reclusion transcribing codices. A commentary on the *Rule of Saint Benedict* is ascribed to him. In 1278 he offered his own work to the compilation of the *Life of Camaldolese Hermits* and it was inserted into Prior General Gerard II's *Constitutions*. Blessed Simon was later entrusted with contributing to the composition of *Book IV On Customs (De Moribus)*, a collection of customs then in force at the Hermitage of Camaldoli which was confirmed by the 1279 General Chapter.

Like his disciple Pellegrine, Simon had a special predilection for chant and beautifully transcribed various psalters and liturgical books for use at the Hermitage, adding the Gregorian notation when necessary. The chroniclers state that they had seen one of these richly embellished psalters of chants in the Hermitage library, but today it is lost.

Blessed Simon greatly loved to pray and he prolonged his prayer for many hours, day and night. He was known for his prudence and his hermit confreres derived much benefit from his wisdom. He died in his hermit cell one year after his dear disciple's death, on September 18, 1292. His bones await the resurrection together with those of Blessed Pellegrine.

III. *Bl. Michael Pini +1522*

A true Florentine, Michael was born to a good religious family in 1440. He received a solid Christian education through which he began to root himself in the principles of a healthy spiritual life. Given his cultural conditions, he was able to study with enthusiasm and considerable success.

Because he had marked moral and humanistic qualities, he was able to be introduced to the Court of Lorenzo De'Medici while he was still young and entrusted with the task of being cup bearer. His gifts endeared him to Lorenzo the Magnificent and he was ordained priest in Florence, with the intention of having him serve as court chaplain.

But the youth's intentions were took him elsewhere. The occasion for a visit to the Hermitage of Camaldoli by Lorenzo the Magnificent suggested to Michael, who was part of the entourage, the path on which he should embark and the choice he must make. He spoke with Prior General Blessed Mariotto Allegri (+1478) who admitted him into the community of Camaldoli. A little later, Michael finally had the joy of realizing his two great aspirations: to live in solitude and to fulfil his deep yearning for contemplation. He lived these years with an ever-growing fervor until, driven by the interior force of the Spirit, Michael requested and obtained reclusion.

Until his death, his hermit cell, which is still preserved, was the stage for his spiritual ascents which fashioned him an authentic servant of the Lord. He fostered a remarkable devotion to the Savior's sacred humanity, which he earnestly contemplated with burning zeal in the mysteries of the crucifixion, death and resurrection. During one of these moments of intense prayer, the devotional institution of the Lord's Crown suggested itself to him as a simple means for stimulating simple souls toward contemplation of the more important periods of Jesus' earthly life. He himself composed one of these Crowns which was even given as a gift to Pope Leo X by Michael's prior. The Pontiff approved of the devotion officially in a Papal Brief on February 18, 1516, in Florence, adding many indulgences to the practice.

There are also accounts of miracles obtained through Blessed Michael's prayers. He was famous for the gift of prophecy and his knowledge of Sacred Scripture. Cardinals Julio De'Medici and Alexander Farnese came to him for advice on a number of occasions. He predicted for each of them their respective rise to the Supreme Pontificate, which actually happened. The former took the name Clement VII (+1534) and the latter, Paul III (+1549). Blessed Michael Pini died in holiness on January 21, 1522, after foreseeing through divine grace the very day and hour of his return to the Father. He earned a reputation for sound sanctity. Altars in some of the Order's churches were dedicated to him.

IV. *Ven. Louis Massei +1679*

Louis was born Charles Massei on May 10, 1622, at Lucca, the first of four sons by the noble patricians, Andrew and Bianca Bernardini. As a monk he took the name Louis.[201] When he was fourteen, a heavy block of marble accidentally fell on his right foot while he was playing in the garden, and a large gash opened up. Two surgical operations did not cure him. In fact, medical bungling meant that Massei would be tormented by pain and a deformed foot for the rest of his life.

At sixteen, he began studies in Bologna. But while he progressed wonderfully in knowledge, his spirit declined. After running around with a circle of friends with loose morals, he let himself get carried into a dissolute experience. The sudden death of a noble patrician he knew proved to be God's means for hoisting him from the abyss into which he had fallen. Weeping bitterly over the Lord's gifts he had squandered, he made a heartfelt return to the Father's arms.

Charles began his new life by renouncing money and thinking seriously about retreating into solitude. He went to Rome at the age of nineteen to seek the advice of his brother Cesare, an Oratorian priest. While he was absorbed in prayer before a crucifix at Saint Paul Outside-the-walls on Good Friday, 1641, he felt the pressing desire not to postpone any longer his decision to enter monastic life. He thought of Camaldoli and went up to the Hermitage, asking to be received. Politely refused because of his lame leg and foot, Charles went back to Rome and got letters of recommendation from Capponi, the Cardinal-Protector of the Camaldolese, who wrote to Prior Jeremiah in support of the twenty–three year-old Massei's request for admission. After overcoming other problems, Charles Massei was welcomed by the hermits of Camaldoli on May 3, 1645, and given the name Louis.

For Louis, these were 'days of salvation and the favorable time.' It was not enough for him merely to live the monastic life, but he committed himself to a permanent process of conversion and penitence, keeping in sight the supreme joys of contemplation. Louis' progress must have been quite famous if, only five years after entering the Hermitage, he was presented to Bishop Salviati of Arezzo for priestly ordination in 1650. This important stage in his life, however great, was not enough to sustain his yearnings for sanctity. The following year, when he was only twenty-nine, he received reclusion in which he persevered until death. And if the criterion for admission into reclusion has always been that of furthering only fervent and observant hermits, Louis was certainly among these. His confreres agreed with his move into reclusion.

As for Louis, he did not disappoint the community's expectations. He began to dedicate himself to prayer and *lectio divina* for up to eighteen hours a day, allowing two hours for labor and four hours for sleep. His cultural background lent itself to intellectual work, so he wrote a tract of his *Injunctives on the Decalogue,* still extant in the Camaldoli archives, along with some homilies which, as we will see, he was assigned to address to the community. What sleep he allowed himself was not taken on the customary mattress of the hermits, but in a chair.

His food regimen seems awesome to us. He ate only unseasoned wild herbs which he grew in a little garden. He never drank wine. Louis continued this regimen for ten years until a serious resurgence of his old illness finally had the prior contemplating Massei's removal from reclusion. But Don Louis did not feel he had to obey because the General Chapter had agreed to his reclusion, an erroneous conviction, and he received a harsh, and correct reprimand from his spiritual director, Landina, the General Superior of the Clerics of Holy Mary of Corte. The good hermit changed his mind and, prostrating himself on the ground, repeatedly begged pardon from the prior, imposing on himself an adequate penance.

Meanwhile, he wasn't getting any better, so a transfer was suggested to the Hermitage of Cortona where the climate was milder and it was thought Louis could benefit from the change. But nothing happened. Another transfer to the Hermitage of Genoa was made, but again nothing changed. Don Louis took the opportunity of returning to ask humbly for his re–entry to Camaldoli as he could no longer hide the fact that he had reached the summit of his calvary. He did return and entered reclusion once again. In supporting this move, the prior believed he was discerning the Lord's will, but he recommended that Louis not return to his wild herbs regimen without adding milk and eggs to the diet. Louis promptly obeyed, but his stomach refused both of these additions, as he systematically regurgitated everything.

Around this time, in addition to the spasms in his ulcerous leg and the penances to which the holy hermit had grown accustomed, Louis suffered a most tedious problem with parasites which bit and ulcerated his flesh. Instead of having recourse to proper remedies, Don Louis considered this development a new means for performing penance, so he lived this authentic martyrdom in silence until his death.

Four years before he died, he was named Lecturer in Theology, an office usually reserved to recluses, to which Massei applied himself with competence. So, he had an opportunity to give his confreres a true service of love and they listened to him. It is said that, speaking in church on the feast of the Assumption, 1678, with Cardinal Nicholas Acciaioli present, the cardinal was astonished by Louis' words and, along with others, was moved to serious compunction.

Louis was very close to Fr. Paul Segneri, the famous Jesuit preacher who came to Louis several times for advice and spiritual direction. Through a gift of the Lord, Louis could foresee that Sister Death was knocking at his door by this time, so he intensified his prayer to ready himself to meet his God. He died in his chair on August 28, 1679, at 9:00 p.m. His friend Paul Segneri, who was then engaged in a mission to the people of Poppi, was among the first, after Louis' own confreres, to go up to the Hermitage to pay homage to the venerable man's remains.

Don Louis Massei had lived fifty-seven years, twenty-eight of which were spent as a hermit and recluse. His remains rest in the Pope's chapel at the Hermitage of Camaldoli.[202]

Bl. Sylvester +1348 and Bl. Paula +1357

Now to two lovable cenobitical figures: a monk and a nun. He was a monastery cook. She was the abbess who had found, in the monks' cook, the father of her soul. Both were in love with God, aflame like two seraphim; both were blessed by the Holy Spirit with great mystical gifts. The Camaldolese monk, Don Zanobi Tantini, wrote their lives in 1394. To be precise, he wrote two versions, one in prose and another in couplets, in a very pleasant and lively thirteenth-century Italian which takes one back to the spontaneous and humble environment of the Franciscan little flowers.[203]

Sylvester was born at Montebonello near Rufina, in the Sieve Valley. He was named Ventura at his baptism. While still young, he lost his entire inheritance for unknown reasons and was reduced to poverty. He went to Florence, thinking he would become a wool-carder. Ventura was no angel. Tantini writes:

> He was arrogant, annoying, problematic and tough; quick and hot-tempered, given to gluttony and drunkenness... dishonest in word and deed, lavish with his property and his life... without restraint; miserably, he let himself be driven to pleasure.

Ventura heard there was a famous preacher at Holy Mary of the Flowers and all of Florence was rushing to hear him.

The preacher was the Dominican friar, Blessed Jordan of Rivalto. Ventura the wool–carder went there more out of curiosity than thirsting for God. But even if he was not searching for God, he discovered that God was waiting for him. He heard one, then another, and still other sermons, until he grew fascinated by Jordan's words which succeeded, little by little, in opening a passage for grace.

> Drawn by efficacious words and other means, he was wounded in his heart and filled with the fear of God, as he began to see the horror of his sins; with sobs, sighs and tears, he began to reflect on lost time and his wicked life.

Grace had broken him. Ventura converted and became a new person. He did not stop listening to Friar Jordan. Sitting diligently at attention in the very first row, he did not blink an eye while the friar's words descended upon him and enkindled him with insatiable fervor. The preacher's great labor made such an impression on him that he too was capable of speaking non-stop for two hours. The holy man needed to refresh himself, so here is what our Ventura did:

> Friar Jordan, having preached much,
> spoke well until he was exhausted.
> He had preached for two hours
> so magnificently that everyone marvelled.
> And Brother Sylvester compassionately
> waited at the foot of the terrace
> and comforting him, had given him
> a small bottle of the best wine.
> The friar enjoyed many gulps.

Brother Sylvester was the name he eventually took as a monk, (he actually had three names). But we should take things in order. His humble act was also pleasing to God, as well as to the poor friar. And God, 'regarded the inner man with affection.' One day while Ventura was going to Orsanmichele near the church of Saint Martin, 'Jesus Christ appeared to him in his crucified form.' Ventura was rapt in ecstasy while love's flame blazed in his heart. He said that the image remained fixed in his mind for eight years and he frequently wept tears of consolation and joy in the Spirit.

Born again to new life and setting aside all trace of his old habits, Ventura sought solitude where he could attend to God alone. He went to a holy man, a certain brother Dino who lived near Castagno in northern Mugello. He told him everything and then asked if he could stay with him. Brother Dino agreed and Ventura took the name Vincenzo. Vincenzo remained with Dino of Castagno only four years. He wanted greater solitude and transferred to another hermitage where he lived seven years with another hermit companion who worked, while Vincenzo immersed himself in prayer.

But one night the poor hermitage was attacked by thieves who took everything from the two hermits, dragged them into the woods and beat them. Now bereft,, and on the advice of a Franciscan friar, Vincenzo understood that the best thing to do would be to place himself under obedience to a superior. He returned to Florence and knocked at the door of the Camaldolese monastery of Holy Mary of the Angels, just outside the Balla Gate (today the Alfani Road). He was welcomed into the 'conversi' monks and renamed Sylvester in 1315.

Assigned to the kitchen, he became the monastery cook for almost the rest of his life. His personal preferences for prayer and meditation remained and, at times, he was so absorbed in God that he would forget he had a pan on the fire 'so that the food was unsalted or smelled smoky; at another time, too strong and had to be taken back.' He humbly admitted his fault in Chapter, asked his confreres for forgiveness and promised to work better while praying less!

But his fervor increased and his familiarity with God grew much more intense. During the hours when he could stay in his cell for prayer, he appeared to be penetrated and pervaded by the Holy Spirit: 'shouting as though enraged, he said *That is he, that is he, that is the one consuming me!'* He also started running through the cloister because he felt a great fire within himself, and 'he would loudly ask everyone he met: *What is God? What is God?'* When none of his confreres had the answer to his question, he ran to Sister Paula, his spiritual daughter, to ask her. She, 'the consort of such an excessive saint, responded: *God is love; he is love!*' And if he happened to hear the monks singing in choir, he would be amazed that 'their hearts were not breaking apart in the sweetness of the psalms.' Even though he was illiterate, he interpreted and explained the hidden mysteries of Sacred Scripture. Sister Paula discoursed learnedly at this source of heavenly wisdom more than anyone else. She was in the habit of saying that while Saint Paul had been snatched up into heaven once, 'Brother Sylvester had been abducted three times. He was inebriated, this man, with the fruitfulness of the Lord's house and drank deeply from the river of divine pleasures. God filled him with the spirit of wisdom and understanding; and he robed him with a stole of honesty and truth.'

Sylvester became the advisor to half of Florence! Brother Simon da Cascia and Brother James Passavanti—both famous preachers—used to consult often with Sylvester to be illuminated on the more difficult points of theology, and they were convinced that 'Sylvester was seated next to the tabernacle of the God of Jacob, near the divine majesty.' Prior General Bonaventure always wanted Brother Sylvester to sit next to him at table whenever he came to the Florentine house, so he could listen to his words. One time, in front of some scholars 'he began to unlock exalted meanings to Sacred Scripture, like a true servant of God.'

Then something quite unusual happened. The monks gathered in Chapter elected Sylvester as their prior. He refused because he was humble and not ordained to the priesthood. So the monks found a way to give him the job without the title. The title went to Don Philip who, according to everyone, did nothing without first consulting Sylvester.

1348 went down in history as a very sad year for Florence. There was a plague which cut down many people, to the point that they no longer knew where to bury the corpses. Sylvester too was struck down. 'He then said a few things joyously, full of holy faith, "Truly, life departs this false, lying, fleeting world and the blessed soul goes to heaven to enjoy eternity." ' Sylvester died on June 9, 1348, at the age of seventy.

> And so he stands in Paradise
> contemplating Christ with the other chosen,
> tasting the food of eternal life,
> with the angels and the saints for eternity,
> singing and rejoicing in the Lord God
> and glowing always with true love.

They say that Sylvester appeared to Sister Paula on the same day of his death, telling her that 'What was freed from the body had been assumed into heaven.'

Paula was born in Borgo Pinti, in the heart of Florence, was baptized 'in beautiful Saint John,' and named Tinga. Her childhood was good: surrounded with kindness and affection by her parents, she loved to play children's games and was properly instructed. She grew up kind and drawn to prayer. We read in her life that she had a vision of the Virgin who suggested that she begin to frequent the monastery of the Angels. When there she met Brother Sylvester and asked him to instruct her in God's way and direct her to the monastic life.

When Paula's father caught an inkling of such plans, he took her to Genoa with him, more out of fear of losing his only daughter than trying to oppose God's will. They stayed there from some time. Only when her father thought she had abandoned thoughts of becoming a nun, he decided to return to Florence. But the idea of monastic life had not left Paula at all, perhaps it had even magnified during her forced absence. Paula returned to Brother Sylvester and made her decision. She went to the nuns of Saint Ursula. Though they allowed her to enter the monastery, they were not particularly interested in this girl, who seemed poorly suited to domestic work. Paula was more Mary than Martha, always loving prayer more and stationing herself at the Lord's feet. Lack of understanding and contradictions welled up in her. Agreeing with Brother Sylvester, Paula left Saint Ursula and, again on his advice, opened a little monastery near Saint Margaret in Cafaggiolo in 1331, where she lived as a nun with Sylvester's sister and another young woman. Paula herself was twenty-two.

With these sisters she could live the type of life she had always craved. Many hours were dedicated to prayer, and they lived on charity for the most part. 'Sister Paula was short and plump, very kind-hearted and loved the Creator fervently. She remained in prayer often.'

The prior of the Angels sometimes sent them food. She placed it on a wooden shelf, but then would pray so long she would forget the food and it would spoil. However, she was 'enraptured and satiated with contemplating Christ Jesus, a true spouse.' Like our Father Saint Romuald, and Brother Sylvester, she had the gift of tears and enjoyed a close familiarity with her Lord. Her life relates that she had many visions, singular graces and mystical gifts: 'and Christ Jesus consoled her so many times, speaking with her, appearing to her, and making her feel indescribable sweetness.'

One of these visions merits specific mention as we have it in her life: 'Another time, wishing to see the Child Jesus, she returned from the parlor and came to her shelf and saw the Child Jesus in his crib above it, and the little one was kicking his legs in the crib. She saw him and said gently, *Oh, my sweet love! Oh! Who has left you here all alone?* So she picked him up reverently and held him in her arms, giving him kisses and hugs devotedly and most lovingly. And for an instant, she saw the Immaculate Virgin Mary waiting for him; suddenly the vision faded away. Thanks be to God!'

Paula did not live very long. She became sick towards the end of 1366 and on January 6, 1367, she died. The monks of the Angels mourned for her, as they had mourned for their saintly brother Sylvester some nineteen years earlier. They received her blessed remains into their monastery so they could preserve them along with those of Brother Sylvester: 'put to rest in the Chapter room with a beautiful Office to the praise and glory of Christ Jesus, to whom be honor and glory forever. Amen!' Neither Sylvester nor Paula had a cultic following, but their names figure into the list of Florence's patron saints, with the title of 'Blessed.' Their bones now rest in the church at Camaldoli.

Two Artists: Lorenzo Monaco and Bartolomeo Della Gatta

These two monks were painters; the former is more famous, but both are excellent. They were educated for the monastic life and pictoral arts in the Florentine monastery of Holy Mary of the Angels. They were not contemporaries. When the second was born, the first had been dead some twenty-three years.

I. Lorenzo, Monaco +1425

What history can tell us is not equal to the celebrity of Don Lorenzo, a gentle monk and most exquisite painter. The chroniclers themselves do not say much more than what George Vasari[204] wrote about him in the sixteenth century. But his many works remain, all splendid and transparent with the purest religiosity. They are indeed the most precious and original document of this Camaldolese monk's heart and talent.

Born in Siena, Peter di Giovanni came with his father to Florence while still a baby. He lived and died there. He became a monk of Holy Mary of the Angels when he was around twenty years old, taking the name Don Lorenzo. Lorenzo had his schooling at the 'Angioli,' as the Florentines referred to the monastery, 'the school of the Lord's service' just as the *Rule* wishes, a school of the finer arts which flourished in the fourteenth century: miniature painting; painting; embroidery; tapestry weaving; transcription of manuscripts. He was an exemplary monk. His gifts of simplicity and lightness of heart helped in acquiring monastic virtues, especially his love of silence and meditation. So he discovered the ideal climate in which his wonderful works of miniatures could flourish, as did his paintings in which Lorenzo transfused his own contemplation of the Christian mystery onto the beautiful faces of Christ, the Virgin and the Saints.

He made his monastic profession on December 10, 1391. From Vasari: 'Don Lorenzo di Giovanni from Saint Michael de'Bisdomini in Florence, formerly called Peter, made his profession in this monastery on December 10, 1391, after completing his novitiate year.' He received minor Orders and became a deacon later on. He did not become a priest.

His refinement and natural gifts steered Lorenzo toward painting and miniature painting.

He did splendid illuminations on manuscript after manuscript, according to the monastery's tradition. He painted on boards; he did fresco-painting. But if he hardly stood out as a miniaturist among his confreres and did not stand up to Gaddi or Starnina as a fresco-painter, he would have the most fortunate hand as a painter on boards... The elegance of the Gothic line beneath his style fashioned it tense and vibrant, like a tone of agony.[205]

Gaddi was his master, the best among Giotto's followers. He was a pupil of Taddeo Gaddi. He was the precursor of Blessed Angelico and later also his disciple. He excelled over all the other mystical painters from the first half of the fifteenth century, except his master. He painted miniatures with finesse.[206]

He came under the influence of Giotto's followers and the School of Siena, and his own painting clearly shows traces of one or the other through whom the painting of Lorenzo Monaco becomes typically thirteenth-century, with that wholly Laurentian note of 'disembodied painting, extremely polished and abstract...considered the epitome of religious painting.'[207] His manner reflects eminently his monastic heart—a man of prayer.

Nine of his frescoes are still preserved in Holy Trinity at Florence. Ten wooden panels remain, the masterpiece of which is *The Coronation of the Virgin* which was painted for his own monastery church and is now admired in the Uffizi Gallery. And there are many manuscript miniatures, a considerable number of which the Laurentian Library of

Florence now preserves. Don Lorenzo died young at the age of only fifty-five. He was buried in his monastery's Chapter room.

II. *Bartolomeo Della Gatta +1502*

A patient monk by nature, a lively and versatile genius,[208] Don Bartolomeo was also a miniaturist, painter, architect, musician and organ builder. He too was a Florentine, born in 1448 and named Peter Antonio Dei. His father was a goldsmith, but he was unable to pass on his art to his three sons because all three became Camaldolese monks. Peter became a monk while still a youth, at Saint Benedict outside the Borgo Pinti Gate. He was given the name Bartolomeo and a little later, as the canons at that time allowed, he made profession. Spending some time in consideration of his talents, his prior entrusted him to their confreres at Holy Mary of the Angels where he studied and assimilated the art of miniature-painting under the master, Julian Amidei, 'a very scholarly painter.'

In 1470 when he was twenty-two and not yet a priest, Bartolomeo was sent to the monastery of Holy Mary in Gradi at Arezzo, where he spent most of the rest of his life. In Arezzo he revealed and exercised his painting skills and architectural talents. The Borgo Sansepolcro and Castiglioni Fiorentino community art gallery of this city (Pinacoteca Comunale), as well as the Cortona e Monte S. Savino, care for many of his better works. He also almost single-handedly frescoed the Saint Peter Piccolo church in Arezzo, but these frescoes were lost during its restoration in the eighteenth century.

Don Bartolomeo's art is known for its delicate coloring, technique, manner and design which reflect the supreme Piero Della Francesca whom Bartolomeo passionately admired. A singular mark of his painting is its finesse and patient touch of the miniaturist, particularly in the little figures on the second floors with certain minor details or memorable refinements of facial expression or folds in clothing.

Bartolomeo went to Rome in 1482, expressly invited there by Perugino and Signorelli then engaged on the colossal work of the Sistine Chapel. He left his own contribution in the frescoes of the *Promulgation of the Law, Death of Moses* (Signorelli) and *Custody of the Keys* (Perugino), in which Bartolomeo painted his self-portrait. He returned to Arezzo after a short priorship in the small monastery of Saint Clement and was elected abbot of Holy Mary in Gradi. Another quality which stood out in Bartolomeo was his musical bent for building church organs with lead pipes, as at Saint Clement. But he also built one with pasteboard at Saint Dominic which Vasari states in his day had "kept soft and gentle".

As an architect, Don Bartolomeo has left a clear example of classic renaissance style in the church of the Annunciation at Arezzo, assisted by two younger men, Antonio (+1534) and Julian (+1516) Sangallo. Bartolomeo died in December, 1491.

Bl. Ambrose Traversari +1439

Ambrose was born in 1386 at Portico di Romagna in the Romagnese Apennines, at the high Montone Valley a few kilometers from the Muraglione Pass. He entered the monastery of Holy Mary of the Angels in Florence when he was fourteen. There he began humanistic studies and on November 5, 1401, made monastic profession. He is probably the most distinguished Camaldolese scholar, able to speak fully and eruditely about both sacred and secular matters. His lively intellect, quick memory, tenacious will and fine taste fashioned him a man of high culture and exquisite sensibility. He learned Greek and perfected his Latin in the monastery where he studied philosophy and theology thoroughly, later becoming a competent master who was known and sought out, without ever sacrificing any of his monastic reserve. He was a fine person, gracious in speech, lucid in his advice, handsome in visage, slender and short of stature.

Ambrose Traversari

Both young and old came to him from all over the Florence of humanistic times, hoping to attain his fineness and command of classical languages, to the point that whoever studied at the school of Don Ambrose could speak Greek and Latin fluently and elegantly.

The gentle monk was at the very core of humanist thought, and he always tried—as did others—to give it a more 'Christian' face. So through the merits of Ambrose, we can speak of a 'Christian humanism,' as distinct from simply classical humanism. Born as a scientific, critical and artistic movement, humanism aspired to raise up the value of classical antiquity. In doing so, humanism closed the medieval period and opened the Renaissance. This cultural movement is of the utmost importance and Traversari is among the most celebrated representatives of its Christian elaboration. Out of the awakening to ancient culture and the knowledge of Greek and Latin classics came the rediscovery of Christian Patristical treasures, both of eastern and western theology. If the reflowering of the taste for, and study of, classical literature was already considered an instrument for the spiritual elevation of humanity (hence the resurgence of the Ciceronian expression *studia humanitatis* = Humanism), there began within humanism an important and sometimes determinant aspect for moral growth beyond the human intellect, under the Christian influence.

A perspective like this prompted Ambrose to dedicate himself to transcribing Saint Athanasius' works and translating Greek Fathers, including Saints John Chrysostom, John Climacus and Ephrem the Syrian. But much greater fame attended his translation of the *Lives of the Philosophers* by Diogenes Laertius. One Cosmas De'Medici who procured Greek, Latin and Hebrew manuscripts for Traversari to transcribe, translate and correct, also entrusted his sons Peter and John to Don Ambrose for their literary and religious education.

In 1431 Ambrose's life took on a fuller dimension. Having passed over the most nourished circles of Florentine scholars, Providence moved Ambrose towards greater heights by making him an intelligent and obedient collaborator of the Pope in the Church's government. Pope Martin V died in 1431 and that same year, Cardinal Gabriel Condulmer was elected Pontiff and took the name Eugene IV. Already the Cardinal Protector of the Camaldolese, the new Pope was a very close friend to Don Ambrose. So he could entrust his Camaldolese friend with responsibility, introducing him into the heart of the ecclesial problems of his day. A letter which Traversari addressed to the newly-elected Pope in which he urges the head of the Church to effect some serious reforms is considered to be what influenced Pope Eugene IV to use the talents of the learned and saintly Camaldolese monk.

But before following our monk in the various delicate tasks which Eugene IV entrusted to his care, we must mention that one of the first interventions of the new Pope vis-a-vis the Camaldolese Congregation was to convoke an extraordinary General Chapter which made timely decisions regarding the Prior General, Don Benedict Lanci, against whom many complaints were being lodged in Rome. Traversari also took part in this Chapter as a delegate of his community, but ended up being elected the new Prior General despite his own reluctance. As he would later say, 'Unfortunately I was elected General and I was not allowed much resistance because I was begged, almost forced, by all the brethren.'

The unanimity for Don Ambrose is evidence of the esteem he enjoyed within the Order which entrusted its destiny and hopes to the earnestness and experience of the monk-scholar. For his part, Ambrose took care not to exercise his delicate service, without taking into account the Gospel saying: *Whoever would be great among you, must be your servant, and whoever would be first among you, must be your slave.*[209] But at the same time, he did not feel like a superior of ordinary administration, so to speak, but one responsible for an entire program of reform and renewal, in the clear knowledge that the serious task asked of him would use up all his energy, and provide a 'bitter chalice' of many disappointments and afflictions. He was very faithful to his program, always saying to others: 'Fear nothing except offending God.'

He gave life to Camaldoli by starting a boarding school for youth interested in monastic life, entrusting their care to the intelligent, wise and competent Mariotto Allegri, theologian and teacher. He brought Mariotto from Saint Justus of Volterra for this purpose. Mariotto succeeded him eventually in governing the Congregation. The school preceded the institution of the seminary which is usually traced back to Saint Charles Borromeo.

Ambrose undertook the task of conducting the canonical visitations of all the Camaldolese monasteries and hermitages with skill and meticulous care, during those hard times when conditions were not the best for getting around. He described this situation in elegant Latin in his *Hodoeporicon,* a voyage journal where, along with references to various situations encountered, the humanist author also makes acute observations about arts and letters. To a great extent, the implementation of his projected reform happened during these visitations.[210]

But the moment arrived when Eugene IV's old friendship with Ambrose reminded him to engage Ambrose in more direct service to the internal Church, which was just as much in need of reform as the Order. The Pope had already convoked a Council which would effect the premises necessary to begin such a serious undertaking.

Martin V had already entrusted to Ambrose the translation of Manuele Caleca's *Against the Errors of the Greeks,*[211] but it was Eugene IV who really made use of Traversari, naming him his nuncio to the Council of Basel. But only twenty out of some six hundred bishops summoned, participated! Owing to the poor attendance, the Council degenerated into a secret meeting pledged more to assure a few interested parties instead of treating the most urgent and general needs of the whole Church. The absurdity affirming the Council's superiority over the Pope immediately predominated. The theory was considered proper even by Cesarini, the Cardinal Legate and Pontifical President, and was carried to the extent of suing the Pope himself.

The vigorous and clearly orthodox reaction of the Camaldolese Prior General who delivered a very erudite speech on August 26, 1435, reclaimed the Pope's supremacy over every Council. Courteous attention was given Ambrose, but the positions taken remained unaltered. The Council was brought to a close. Giving in at last to Traversari's patient and delicate mediation, the Cardinal Legate withdrew his support for the claim. But they still had to get Emperor Sigismund to support the position taken. A new diplomatic mission entrusted to Prior Ambrose by the Pope also reached its desired end.

After clearing away these obstructions from the scene, the Council transferred to Ferrara and its most important aim became the union of the Greek and Latin Churches. Ambrose took part there with his same assignment. But here his role became even more determinant because of his perfect knowledge of Greek which allowed direct personal contacts with the Greek Fathers; Ambrose functioned as interpreter. His own translations had already put him in a position of being quite familiar with the theology of the Greek Fathers of the Church; this too was very important and decisive for the Council's conclusions. Historians of this event see Ambrose as the soul of Ferrara's judgment. All this is still more appreciable if we realize that, at the Council and in its unwinding, Ambrose dedicated himself to translating those Greek texts which he considered useful for the dialogue between the two Churches, even though he had to work through the nights.

Certainly this was exhausting. But he was later entrusted with the noblest task of all: to draft the Bull *Laetentur coeli* in Greek and Latin versions, through which the union of the two Churches was confirmed. This Bull was proclaimed at Florence on July 6, 1439, in the Cathedral of Holy Mary del Fiore, which was already by that time crowned with the splendid, elegant cupola of Brunelleschi. Gentle Ambrose found himself at the center of a triumph, but his innermost joy was for his Mother, the Church, who would no longer be represented with ripped robes.

Another flood of hope poured into hearts, especially Eugene IV's who had already considered honoring the Camaldolese Prior General's work with the cardinal's crimson. But the Lord was calling Ambrose to his own reward. Don Ambrose Traversari died suddenly on October 21, 1439, aged fifty-three. Everyone mourned his loss. Eugene IV mourned him, "Ambrose, my son, who has wrested you from me? Who has put out the Church's light so quickly?" But his own Order mourned him more and rightly so, because they were now deprived of so excellent a leader. For the Camaldolese, however, there remains the shining example and rich life of virtue of their brother whose cultic liturgy recognized by the Apostolic See they confidently await.[212]

Traversari's literary output found its greatest expression in his letters with a fairly comprehensive network of correspondents, comprising particularly his contemporary humanists. The recent centenary celebrations of his birth, 1986-1987, saw a series of important conferences on the person and works of Traversari.[213]

Fra. Mauro the Cosmographer +1459

We now move from Florence to Venice. Saint Michael of Murano was a Camaldolese monastery from 1212 onwards. The church which is older, was given by Bishop Mark of Nicola to the monk Albert, who took possession of it in the name of Prior General Guido II. The monastery rose a few years later and the church, which was rebuilt to suit the needs of a monastic community, was consecrated in 1221 by Cardinal Ugolino—later Pope Gregory IX—who had already been a guest at the Hermitage of Camaldoli. Fra. Mauro, the famous cosmographer, became a monk here.

Mauro's history is largely concerned with his designing geographical projections and constructing splendid world maps. We know nothing about his birthplace, nor anything prior to his monastic life. We find him at Saint Michael: bent over parchment, intent on his cartography. We do not know if he had a master teach him, or if he was self-taught in this art.

In the archives at Murano there is a gilded copper commemorative medallion made by the monastic chroniclers to reproduce on the press at page 256 of Tome VII of the Annales, which reads, in the round, *Frater Maurus. Sancti Michaelis. Moranensis. De Venetiis. Ordinis. Camaldulensis. Chosmographus. Incomparabilis!* The attribute *incomparabilis* points out the value placed on this monk's work and the fame he deserves, so that historians began habitually to refer to him as 'Fra. Mauro the cosmographer' or 'Fra. Mauro the Camaldolese.' It was written,

> His entire study was to delineate and bring to perfection geographical maps, keeping himself informed, with the greatest possible precision, on the discoveries being made by Italian and foreign explorers.[214]

He lived in the time of the great navigators: Marco Polo had died in 1324 and the echo of his undertakings was still very much alive in Fra. Mauro's day; Christopher Columbus died in 1506. Fra. Mauro took his inspiration to sketch the 'India terra' from Polo. For his part, Columbus later took good information from one of Mauro's planispheres and from that, sketched (under the commission of King Alfonso V of Portugal) where to investigate and attempt a voyage to India by maintaining a westward course instead of a southeasterly one, as was customary at that time.

Today we can still admire two of his world maps: one is the map of 1457 mentioned above, preserved at Lisbon; the other map dated 1459 can be found at Saint Mark's Library in Venice.[215] Both maps, with diameters of about five feet, are laid on the finest parchment, showing how the patient monk of Murano wanted the finesse and elegance of a miniature. Still today Mauro's works display brilliant gold and pigments.

We know nothing more of the incomparable Mauro's history. He died in 1459. We should add only one other pleasant note. When astronauts first landed on the moon in July, 1969, the reporter mentioned many times 'the lunar crater of Fra. Mauro.' There were many asking who this Fra. Mauro might be. The answer is exactly the Camaldolese cosmographer of the fifteenth century. His name had been given that crater because he was the one who had located it. Not a note of great importance, perhaps, but it contributes toward making the name of this humble and intelligent monk who left behind signs of an active life while living in the silence of a monastery on an island in the Venetian Lagoon re-emerge from the distant past.[216]

Nicholas Malerbi +1481

This monk's renown derives from an innovation in the field of books which ascribes to him the first translation of the Bible into Italian. A few copies of this work still exist, which are inscribed (probably by the hand of a confrere or disciple):

> Bible worthily translated into the vernacular by the brilliant Venetian religious, Nicholas of Malerbi, the most reverend abbot of Saint Michael of Lemmo monastery. Two volumes in folio with two columns. Venice, with typeface by Vendelino da Spira.

More than thirty editions of this Bible had been done by 1567, a little more than eighty years later—surely a sign of its welcome by the well–educated and ecclesiastics. The celebrated literary critic, Tiraboschi, made this observation:

> A very distinct mention should be made of Nicholas Malermi (sic), or Malerbi, from Venice, a Camaldolese monk who is the first to give us the entire Sacred Scriptures translated into the Italian language.[217]

Nicholas was born at Venice in 1422 and entered Saint Michael of Murano when he was forty-eight. He later became abbot of Saint Michael of Lemmo, but the work which made him famous was done beforehand, while he spent time at Saint Matthias on the island of Murano, working there for some eight months. He died at the age of fifty-nine in the year 1481, after spending eleven years as a monk and monk-abbot. [218]

Four Representatives of the Sciences: Edward Baroncini, Guido Grandi, John Benedict Mittarelli & Anselm Costadoni.

I. Edward Baroncini +1741

Edward was a wonderful example of the hermit, shining in his holiness of life and doctrine. He was born at Avignon in 1655, but of a Florentine family. His father Vincent, a patrician, sent his son for studies at the University of Pisa, where he studied to his advantage. After that, Francis (his baptismal name) decided to enter ecclesial life. He became a priest and later, a canon of the metropolitan at Holy Mary of the Flowers. A subsequent visit to Camaldoli inspired him to interrupt his ecclesiastical career to become a hermit. He professed vows at the age of thirty-five in 1690.

Named librarian and archivist, he was able to put his intellectual and doctrinal capacities to good use. A scholar, he was an expert in Greek and Latin, and also enjoyed a remarkable competence in paleography and bibliography. 'He diligently examined more than three hundred and fifty manuscripts, five thousand parchments and thousands of various volumes.'[219] He wrote *Chronicon Camalduli,* an historical/critical work covering seven centuries of Camaldolese history (1012-1712), still unpublished but from which the Chroniclers themselves obtained much of their information.

The diligence and scrupulous attention Baroncini put into his scientific research can be seen above all in his monastic endeavors. His contemporaries and historians have recognized in him a real example of holiness. Austere and cheerful at the same time, he was a penitent and a man of vigorous interior life which he nourished with intense prayer. He was Prior of the Hermitage and then, Elder Father of the whole Congregation, an office from which he repeatedly asked to be released so he could more freely dedicate himself to his studies and spiritual growth. His final years brought on annoying illnesses which purified him within, preparing him to meet the Lord. He died at the age of eighty-seven on August 23, 1741.

II. *Guido Grandi +1742*

Guido was born at Cremona in 1671. When he was sixteen, he became a monk at Saint Apollinare in Classe at Ravenna, where he professed vows three years later. Amazed by his capabilities, his superiors wanted him to study letters and philosophy, but Don Guido possessed specific gifts for experimental sciences and mathematics, in which disciplines he revealed his greatness. In 1700 he was asked to accept a professorship at the University of Pisa for the chair of physics and mathematics, a post which he held for most of his lifetime. His fame stems from some discoveries he made in the field of mathematics and geometry. He studied thoroughly and drafted a geometrical demonstration for Huygens' theories of logarithms, a squaring of the circle, hyperbole, and disquisitions on infinity.

Guido also studied historical figures and wrote the *Dissertationes Camaldulenses* (Lucca, 1707), with the aim of taking up again some historical/critical controversies of Camaldolese history, tracking them down and solving them. His objectiveness and respect for the truth make his lack of scruples in transcribing historical facts stand out, as he amplified and, in some cases, altered documents. One might think that doing such could have been induced by a lack of good intentions toward his Order, to the detriment of truth. If we ought to say that Grandi showed himself a person of truly brilliant capacity in the experimental field of mathematics and geometry, we cannot say the same about his capacity in the historical/critical realm!

The Pope and Grand Duke of Tuscany made use of Abbot Guido Grandi in a number of projects to do with hydraulics, with fortuitous results. Endowed with sound moral gifts, he was a man of remarkable piety, which won him the election as Abbot General of the Congregation. He died in Pisa on July 4, 1742.

III. *John Benedict Mittarelli +1777*

Passing over these pages and the accompanying notes, one cannot miss the initials: *AA.CC.* The reader has understood that this is about the Camaldolese chroniclers, or annalists. Now we have the opportunity to become acquainted with the names and works of the authors of this *historicum monumentum* of fundamental interest for Camaldolese history. These are two learned and holy monks, both professed monks of Saint Michael of Murano who became abbots of that community: Don John Baptist Mittarelli and Don Anselm Costadoni.

If it is true that studious people's worth is linked to their genius and perspicacity, it is just as true, for a complete judgment, that it is necessary to measure the usefulness of their output! Reflecting on the historical, critical and paleographical value of these two chroniclers, we must state no other scholarly and erudite Camaldolese work is as useful as the work accomplished by Mittarelli and Costadoni. The eighteenth century in which they lived and worked is the century of great exegetical/ critical and historical/literary editions which attracted the attention of the scholars to the number of distinguished historians and even more, to their monumental works. The name Muratori suffices for the lay sector; in the ecclesiastical, especially Benedictine sector, we must mention the famous Maurist editions which claim the most celebrated names like Mabillon, Martene, Montfaucont, and the Italian productions of Ughelli, Quirini, Gattola and, not the least, Mittarelli and Costadoni.

John Benedict Mittarelli is the real father of Camaldolese history, the one who carried the greater weight in the compilation and redaction of the *Annales* through his critical acumen, patient research and composition. For his part,

Anselm Costadoni invested his own diligence and skill in the massive undertaking of compiling the appendices and various indices of the richest nomenclature.

Mittarelli was born in Venice on September 2, 1707. He owed his scholastic and literary education to Canon John Oker and later, the Jesuits, who were his masters of philosophy. Finished with his philosophical course, he became a monk at Saint Michael of Murano, where he made monastic profession on November 14, 1723. Taking his remarkable intellect into consideration, his superiors wanted John Benedict to embark on theological studies at Florence and Rome. His time in Rome accorded him the opportunity to develop a friendship with Cardinal Rezzonico (later Pope Clement VIII), and his Secretary of State, Cardinal Archinto. The Congregational Diet of 1732 recalled him to Saint Michael as Lecturer in Philosophy and Theology. He became the Novice Master nine years later. Finally, in 1760, the brethren chose him as their abbot. Just five years later, the General Chapter elected him Abbot General of the entire Congregation.

In his capacity as General, John Benedict conducted himself with wisdom and diligent mindfulness for five years and, when his term had expired, he insistently asked to be excused so he could attend to the abbacy of his own monastery on Murano. He remained there until he died on the afternoon of August 14, 1777, while his monks were chanting First Vespers of Mary's Assumption into heaven.

Besides the *Annales,* his scientific output included an ascetical treatise dedicated to his novices, some orations, various works of an historical nature and some lives of saints. He was able to dedicate the best of his experience and teaching to the *Annales* project, scrupulously examining a considerable quantity of authentic documents and historical/hagiographical books already published or in manuscript form, travelling to consult all the archives of the Camaldolese hermitages and monasteries—including the extinct ones—undertaking the burden of many difficult moves from one place to another. He copied Bulls, diplomatic deeds, and documents about donations and administrations, enlarging his own investigation to include various relations different people and monasteries had with the outside. During Lent, 1755, six years after embarking on this enormous task, he had the justified satisfaction of seeing the publication of Volume I of the *Annales Camaldulenses,* at Venice, using the typeface of John Baptist Pasquali *Superiorum venia et privilegio.* The remaining eight volumes demanded eighteen years of work, the final Appendix being printed four years before his death.

His work was performed with scrupulous competence when quoting documents and settling controversial questions. In its own genre, Mittarelli's work is held as a typical example. Scholars of his day universally received it favorably, considered by some to be close to that more extensive work of Mabillon. He received a Brief of Encouragement and Commendation from Pope Benedict XIV. His confreres wanted to mint a medallion of recognition with the inscription:

Annalium Camaldulensium conditori et patri

Decem viri Camaldulenses D.D.A. 1765.

The *Annales* begin with the year 907, held at that time to be the year of Saint Romuald's birth, and they end with the year 1764. They were written in beautiful Latin: clear, elegant and serious. Cross–references of dates and names in the margins facilitate reference work. The entire work numbers seven thousand and thirteen pages in folio, and quotes from five hundred and nine Papal Bulls, very many Briefs, and two thousand four hundred and eighty notary's deeds and maps.

But a final word must be said about the spiritual gifts for which the monk Don John Benedict Mittarelli truly endeared himself to God and humanity. His intellectual capacity never lead him to feel superior to others. He had a docile nature, open to encounter—a courteous trait for which he was well loved by his confreres and whoever had any dealings with him. By nature, he was reluctant to accept any dignity but when his brethren wanted him as their superior, he showed his eminent gifts of discretion and spiritual fatherhood. He learned to harmonize culture with the needs of a serious asceticism, fashioning him a man of profound interior life.

IV. *Anselm Costadoni +1785*

Having said all that, we cannot leave the other chronicler in the shadows, Don Anselm Costadoni who was a most worthy confrere of Mittarelli. He was second, only in age, and though he was younger, he had the temperament of the impassioned and patient researcher. Costadoni was the true diligent collaborator, keen and ever as valuable as Don John Benedict in the tenacious work of investigations.

Costadoni was also a Venetian, born on October 6, 1714. When he was eighteen, he became a monk at Murano where he professed vows on August 26, 1731. He finished his philosophical and theological training, having had Mittarelli as Lecturer and deriving the greatest benefit from the experience, until he gained the reputation for being one of the most scholarly people in Venice. He also had a genius for historical studies and, beyond being a great help to Mittarelli in the compilation of the *Annales*, he wrote a large body of work. The publications consist of four works on philosophical arguments and some lives of saints and scholars. But the majority of his writings remain unpublished. Among them we must mention the *Anecdota Camaldulensia:* twelve manuscript volumes in folio which are waiting for the diligent mind and skill of the enthusiastic connoisseur who will edit them. Regarding his contribution to the *Annales Camaldulensis,* Don Anselm proved his worth in the compilation of the Appendices. He succeeded Mittarelli in the role of abbot at Saint Michael, while the latter served as Abbot General. A humble and modest person, he was conspicuous for his love of prayer and diligent and earnest in ascetical commitment. He died on January 22, 1785, at the age of seventy-one.

A Camaldolese on the Throne of Peter: Gregory XVI +1846

We end this survey of famous names, the living patrimony of the Camaldolese family, with a son of Saint Romuald called by God to pastoral service as the supreme Head of the Church.[220]

Bartholomew Cappellari was born at Belluno on September 18, 1765. When he was eighteen, he became a monk of Saint Michael of Murano where Don Anselm Costadoni was abbot at the time. He made profession on August 23, 1786, taking the religious name Maur. He had a confrere four years younger, Don Placid Zurla,[221] later Cardinal and Vicar for the Rome diocese, with whom Don Maur formed a friendship, either through their common love of theology or out of sincere and animated esteem.

After his priestly ordination, Cappellari was put in charge of teaching theology and philosophy to the young monks of his monastery. Elected Procurator General in 1795, he transferred to Rome. His new duties did not hinder him from his favorite studies, so that he was able to publish his work *The Triumph of the Holy See* in 1799 at Rome. Following a typically scholastic / apologetical methodology common within contemporary theological research, he wrote about the immutability of Church government and papal infallibility which was later defined by Vatican Council I.[222]

In 1800 Cappellari was named abbatial Vicar of Saint Gregory al Celio[223] and in 1805, abbot. Three years later he was abbot at Saint Michael of Murano where he stayed until 1814 when he again returned to Rome in the capacity of abbot of Saint Gregory. During this second Roman abbacy, he was named Consulter of the Holy Office, Propagation of the Faith, and Extraordinary Ecclesiastical Affairs. On March 13, 1826, Pope Pius VIII created him cardinal, entrusting to him the task of Prefect for the Propagation of the Faith.

Upon the death of Pope Pius VIII, Cardinal Maur Cappellari was elected Pope on February 2, in the conclave

St. Gregory al Cielo in Rome

of 1831, taking the name Gregory XVI. He was sixty-six and had been a Camaldolese monk for forty-five years. He ruled the See of Peter for fifteen years until June 2, 1846. It is beyond the scope of these notes to give a critical and detailed assessment of the Pontificate of Gregory XVI. We refer you to the two large volumes of the *Miscellanea* containing full, documented studies, published in the first Centenary of the Pope's death (1946-1947).[224]

These objective studies have rescued and vindicated (one hopes definitively!) the character and influence of Pope Cappellari. For superficial notions based on the incomplete and sometimes biased information to which we had grown accustomed, painted Cappellari as reluctant to try anything new, and even sometimes, as an obscurantist. A subtle, biased satire (we are in the times of Gioacchino Belli, +1863, and Giuseppe Giusti, +1850) contributed to the distortion, resulting in our image of Gregory XVI being disfigured and debased. It is astonishing that this judgment of Cappellari as a pontiff hostile to the progress, was maintained by those who espoused liberalism —for the most part, Freemasons—a stance which was fashionable in a large part of civil and political society in those days. The various patriotic movements aiming at the unification of Italy found in Pope Gregory, it is true, a man who was not disposed to renounce a patrimony not his own—the Pontifical State—to defend which he also had recourse to the direct intervention of Austria. But it was also a matter of understanding that, for a pope, what was at stake in the final analysis was the defense of the proper rights usually and naturally identified with the Church's rights—something being reread in the mentality of the times—not at all insinuating the unconditional sentence.

Parallel to views like these, however, remains the ensemble of apostolic interventions, those of wise and learned people, those of a pope—the latest pope, a monk—peacefully vying for a worthy place among the series of Roman pontiffs. As Vicar of Christ, he knew how to do his part, not an insignificant thing, undertaking first of all the

the development and care of the patrimony of faith transmitted by the Apostles. We infer this from three encyclicals in which Pope Cappellari, provoked by serious doctrinal problems, principally explains and exercises his apostolic mandate.

The fifteen years of his pontificate carry the sign of timely interventions in defense of the faith against a series of controversies: doctrinal, heretical movements and schismatics. In one of his encyclicals he took position against the notorious Congressus Badesis, formed for the most part by laity who aimed at subordinating the Church to the State. His encyclical *Mirari vos* of August 15, 1832, had greater resonance in speaking against the political and religious liberalism which had its most tenacious spokesman in Lamennais, with the consequent judgment of the errors contained and published by *L'Avvenir.* The third encyclical, contains some specific religious rebukes, and vindicates the just rights of the social order. It is in this encyclical that Gregory pronounces against slavery which was still being practiced during the nineteenth century in some western states of Africa and in America.

Gregory knew he had to assume positions equally clear and timely regarding ecclesiastical liberalism aiming at rescuing the 'national' churches for the unifying center of Rome, as he did against Hermes' rationalism. He also gave his full support and authorization to the foundation of the Catholic University of Malines in an Apostolic Letter addressed to the city's archbishop.

A particularly distinctive mark of Gregory's pontificate was his great love for the Missions. Already as Cardinal Prefect for the Propagation of the Faith, he had given a strong thrust to the reorganization of missionary activity through well considered criteria for the choice of bishops, liturgical/sacramental practices, solving jurisdictional problems, and the administration of ecclesiastical districts. Once pope, the dynamism of the mission cause assumed dimensions which had never before been reached. He founded many new missions with about seventy new dioceses and apostolic vicars. He named one hundred and ninety-five missionary bishops, among whom were the great Cardinal Massaia and Saint Justin De Jacobis. Pope Cappellari was also an passionate supporter of ecumenism, undertaking the cause for the union of the Oriental Churches of the various rites. Particular emphasis was given his 'Instruction on the clergy and the indigenous hierarchy' and his apostolic firmness regarding the so–called 'Goa' schism.

As Head of State in legislative matters, he announced the promulgation of 'Organic regulation of penal procedure' on November 5, 1831, and "Legislative and judicial regulation for civil affairs' coming into force for the entire territory of the Pontifical State with *Motu proprio* of November 10, 1834.

In the area of culture and the arts, Pope Cappellari is recognized for his good service in founding the Gregorian Egyptian Museum at the Vatican, the Etruscan Museum and that of the Lateran, preceding the latter with a careful restoration of the Lateran Palace, completely restoring it to its original forms. He reorganized the Vatican art gallery and the Arazzi Gallery. He also wanted to restore the transept of the Basilica of Saint Paul Outside–the–Walls, which had been destroyed by an enormous fire. The monks of Camaldoli gave the pope all the needed timber for the new beams. He fostered very interesting archeological excavations and the restorations of renowned structures, such as: the Colosseum, the Arch of Titus, the Arch of Septimius Severus, as well as the Portico of the Temples of Antoninus and Faustina, the Foca Column, the remains of the Temple of Concordia and Vespasian, and important excavations on the Roman Forum.

In conclusion, a quick mention of his lifestyle is in order. Educated and formed in the school of the Lord's service at Saint Michael of Murano, he found it natural when he was pope to pursue his monastic customs, careful not to sacrifice anything in his interior and exterior attitudes toward a simple lifestyle, conforming to the ascetical and familiar spirit of his monastic profession. He had a strong temperament, but was averse to imposing himself. The fear of God usually presided in his decisions and life-choices. He was humble and gracious with all, averse to seeking vain popularity, and somewhat withdrawn. However, he knew how to be witty in a wholesome way, rendering him lovable in his interpersonal relations. He always rose early in the morning so he could have the time and possibility to dedicate himself to God and prolong his prayer.

Gregory was ready to die on June 2, 1846. He welcomed death with the simplicity and monastic humility with which he had always lived:"I want to die as a monk, not as a sovereign."

•

Here ends our list of historical figures whose holiness and teaching are praised by the Camaldolese family. Obviously, they are not the only ones, but it seems to us they are the most expressive. Put next to one another, they offer a panorama of the whole where the pluralism of various approaches expresses the moral richness of a venerated tradition.

five:

Camaldolese Nuns

Communities of women are also represented within the reforming ambit of St. Romuald. As a matter of fact, according to chapters thirty-five and sixty-three of the *Life of Romuald,* we know that the Saint was involved with at least two communities of holy virgins. Returning to some of Peter Damian's remarks about Romuald's stay at Valdicastro, we have noted many of the Saint's actions in setting up options for bishops, priests and laity to return to a life worthy of their vocation.[225] We simply need to add that, in this area of reform, the foundation of a monastery of women consecrated to the Lord (*i.e.* nuns) was introduced in the neighborhood of Valdicastro.

We know that this monastery was not the only one. In a later period, probably while he was staying at the Hermitage of Vivo at the base of Amiata,[226] Romuald considered 'building a monastery for women servants of God in Valbona.'[227]—a place still not clearly determined. According to Peter Damian, the proposal of the man of God did not please some disciples, who only later shared the view of the Master and the other brethren.

Beyond these two instances, the *Life of Romuald* gives us no more information, but in a text from the *Liber tramitis,*[228] we notice that Romuald, 'a wondrous monk,' had various opportunities to build other feminine monastic communities. Unfortunately, neither their names nor their localities have come down to us. However, though information is scarce, it permits us to think that in some sense a tradition had already been established by this time within the circle of the Romualdian movement.

111

Actually, in 1085, a little over fifty years after the reformer's death, the feminine Camaldolese institution found a new champion in Blessed Rudolf IV, Romuald's successor at Camaldoli.[229] He founded the monastery of Saint Peter a Luco at Mugello in the Florentine diocese. There were others too: Saint Christina of Stifonte, or Settefonti, near Bologna (1099); Saint John the Evangelist of Pratovecchio in Casentino (1143); from which depended for a while another monastery of nuns, Saint Mary of Rosano near Pontassieve in the diocese of Fiesole.[230]

Camaldolese history mentions the existence of other 'double' monasteries in the eleventh and fifteenth centuries, where monks and nuns lived in different sections. These were: The monastery of Saint Mary in Avesa near Verona; Saint Christine in the area of Treviso, where a holy monk, Saint Parisio (+1267) was confessor to those nuns for thirty years; Saint Mary of Porcilia near Padua; and Saint Eustachium in Imola. These monasteries had a common church where the monks and nuns gathered for liturgical prayer. Some of the monks were in charge of the spiritual and monastic formation of the nuns.[231]

We also know of at least one monastery of women where a type of eremitical observance was in force, the monastery of Saint Margaret in Cafaggiolo at Florence, where Blessed Paola[232] lived and was dependent upon Holy Mary of the Angels.[233] This was in 1345.

As far as dependency of the feminine monasteries is concerned, arrangements varied. Usually the feminine monastery was under another monastery or hermitage of monks, but sometimes it was directly under the Prior General. Still others found themselves under the jurisdiction of a diocesan bishop.

Today the norm is the one given in Canon Law for almost all monasteries of nuns, which provides that the Camaldolese nuns be subject to the bishop of the diocese in which their monastery is located. Attending to the details of Canon Law, however, and presuming the consent of the Congregation's General Chapter, such a monastery may choose to place itself directly under the jurisdiction of the Prior General.[234]

The bond between the feminine monasteries and the Camaldolese Congregation stems from their identical monastic profession according to the *Rule of Saint Benedict* and the Camaldolese Statutes, with particular customs appropriate to each monastery. The tenor of life is also very similar. There is an accentuation of contemplation as the Rule and tradition suggest, but also a wise attention paid to hospitality, studies, asceticism and, in some cases, to internal activity such as nursery schools and the care of the elderly.

Even recent Camaldolese history speaks to us of 'recluse' nuns for whom the criteria provided by the Constitution for recluse hermits are adapted. Our limits do not permit us to give a complete listing of the Camaldolese nuns, and with a certain regret, we limit ourselves to recalling a few of the of the most noteworthy, some of whom we remember liturgically:

Bl. Joan da Bagno of Romagna (+1105)

Bl. Lucy of Settefonti (Stifonte), Bologna (+1149)

Bl. Maria da Pisa, wife and recluse (+1200)

Bl. Buona di Sant'Anna, Pisa (+1207)

Bl. Wiliana, foundress of a hospice for women, Pisa (+1240)

Bl. Juliana (+1262)

Bl. Gerarda, oblate, Pisa (+1269)

Bl. Elisabeth Salviati, Buldrone (+1520)

Bl. Madeleine di Luco (+1518)

Ven. Maria Debora, philosopher and poetess (+1675)

Ven. Leticia Basilanti of Sant'Archangelo di Romagna (+1700)

Ven. Crocifissa Veraci, stigmatist and mystic, Pratovecchio (+1822)

Ven. Scholastica Laderchi, Faenza (+1864)

Sr. Paola Michelini, friend and contemporary of Saint Gemma Galgani—both spiritual daughters of Msgr. John Volpi, Arezzo (+1964)

We have mentioned only some of the figures. The majority have names linked to their own monasteries and are remembered devotionally. They have left examples of the gifts of generosity and perseverance, making their lives a constant act of thanksgiving to God in (sometimes heroic) sacrifice, and in the eloquence of silence in open dialogue with their Divine Spouse.

Today the Camaldolese women live in seven Italian monasteries, and one each in Poland, France, Tanzania, Brazil, India and America.

six:

Two Famous Monasteries

I. *Saint Michael of Murano*

Murano is the principal island in a group of islands of the Venetian Lagoon, famous for its production of valuable glassware. A small church dedicated to Saint Michael the Archangel had existed there for some time before 1212. In that year the Camaldolese appeared, Bishop Marco di Nicola entrusted the care of the church to a certain monk Albert, who took charge of it in the name of Prior General Guido. A little later, a monastery was built next to the church, with Albert as its prior. Some years passed and Albert began the construction of a larger church. It was consecrated by Cardinal Ugolino De' Conti Segni (later Pope Gregory IX), whom we have already seen stay at the Hermitage of Camaldoli.

Further reconstructions carried out during the beginning of the fourteenth and throughout the fifteenth century, gave the building the lines and characteristics of the Lombard Renaissance style, which remain to this day. From time to time, the sacred edifice was enriched by the very beautiful panels of Cima da Conegliano, Palma and Giovanni Bellini. The works of the latter artist can now be found in the Berlin and Dresden museums.

The very beautiful cloister, still preserved in its original outlines, seems to date back to a little before 1300. The Doges of Venice always held the monastery of Murano in high esteem, endowed it and engendered great respect for the monks. Doge Peter Ziano stands out as being particularly lavish with various privileges and gifts for this cenobium.

THE MONASTERY OF ST. MICHAEL OF MURANO

ANNALES CAMALDULENSES 1755

Certainly before the fourteenth century, the monastery was enriched with a rare and precious relic, a Byzantine reliquary of the Holy Cross which some thieves had stolen in Constantinople, presumably around the year 1250. It remained at Saint Michael of Murano until 1810. Today it is jealously guarded in the Hermitage of Fonte Avellana.

With the passage of time, the prestige of the cenobium of Murano grew considerably, so much so that it annexed the other monasteries of the Lagoon: Saint Michael of Lemmo, Saint Mary of Mandria, Montecroce, Saint Mary of Porcilia, and Saint Martin of Oderzo.

Sanctity of life blossomed particularly in Blessed Peter Sardo (+1407), Blessed Eusebius Spagnolo (+1502) and others. Saint Michael is believed to be the first Camaldolese community to have the right to elect its own prior without the customary presence of the Congregation's Prior General. This privilege was granted the monastery in 1407 by Pope Gregory XII.

Among Murano's monks were students of great repute in the sacred sciences, letters, philosophy and the arts. They made their monastery a noted center of culture. Other monks were elevated to ecclesiastical dignity and rendered pastoral service to the Church. A fine school of miniature–painting flourished there for some centuries; there were many monks devoted to this most delicate art, as well as to the copying of manuscripts. Many people availed themselves of their skills and learned the manner of illuminating manuscripts and parchments. We have already spoken of Fra Mauro, the incomparable cosmographer, who was the most noted alumnus of this school.[235] So too, see the entries on Don Nicholas Malerbi, Abbot John Benedict Mittarelli and Abbot Anselm Costadoni[236] as exponents of the sciences.

We should also mention other luminaries of Saint Michael. Don Maur Lapi (+1478) was a man of holy life and the author of ascetical works. Don Maffeo Gherardo (+1492), was a cardinal and Patriarch of Venice. Don Peter Delfino (+1525), was the abbot of the monastery and later

Prior General. His hundreds of letters in pure and elegant Latin, gathered in an interesting collection, attest to his learning. Don Angelo Calogera (+1766), was learned in sacred and secular disciplines, and the compiler of many booklets on questions of sacred doctrine and secular sciences. Then there were Don Antony Gardin (+1800), Bishop of Crema; Don Placid Zurla (+1834), theologian and Cardinal Vicar of Rome; Don Maur Cappellari (+1846), theologian, apologist and Supreme Pontiff;[237] and lastly, Don Peter Canale (+1851).

In 1612 Saint Michael of Murano found itself the head of another autonomous congregation, after a whole series of events and internal conflicts which caused the entire Camaldolese Congregation to suffer. The new Congregation became known as the Camaldolese Cenobites, it was broken away from Camaldoli and given its own Constitutions and regimen, under the direct jurisdiction of an Abbot General.

Napoleon, then Lord of Venice for some four years, suppressed this illustrious monastery in 1810, unfortunately marking the end of it. Murano was never returned to the Camaldolese, despite the influential mediations of Cardinals Placid Zurla and Maur Cappellari.[238]

II. *Holy Mary of the Angels*

In Florence, one simply used 'The Angels' in reference to the monastery of solitaries of Cafaggiolo, just outside the wall at Balla Gate. A very modest hermitage, it rose around 1295, out of the generosity of Br. Guido of Arezzo (+1294). According to Vasari,[239] Guido was a member of the Order of Holy Mary Mother of God, or so-called Knights of Our Lady. After visiting the famous monastery in the mountains of the high Casentino and edified by the holiness and industriousness of those hermits, the native of Arezzo decided to donate a considerable amount for the construction of a hermitage elsewhere, under a similar observance to that of the Hermitage of Camaldoli. He thought of Florence,

HOLY MARY OF THE ANGELS IN FLORENCE

ANNALES CAMALDULENSES 1764

already famous as a center of culture and the arts, and which had stood out at various times in the past for its good will toward Camaldoli.

In a few years, the humble Hermitage of Cafaggiolo assumed the dimensions of a large monastery, and still other donations rendered possible the excellent architectural work of Florentine masters. The title 'Holy Mary of the Angels' was given the church which, though not large was very elegant. John and Gerard, hermits of Camaldoli, were designated supervisors over these works by Prior General Fridiano during the foundation year. A peculiarly Camaldolese ambience was adopted there, and the monks of 'The Angels' were able to observe a very strict cloister, calling themselves *inclusi* or *reclusi* and never going beyond the monastery walls.

A few decades later, a wonderful school of fine arts entirely worthy of Florence began to flourish at the monastery. An intelligent prior, Don Philip Nelli (+1351), sent for some of the most talented Florentine and Tuscan artists, beginning a tradition that continued until the seventeenth century.[240]

For their part, the monks showed themselves to be on a level with such a wealth of artists, drawing considerable profit from the arrangement. Some of these monks became masters in their own right and had their own schools. We have already spoken of Lorenzo Monaco[241] and his workshop for painting and miniature painting. Others who should be mentioned are Don Jacopo the Florentine, Don Sylvester, Don Simon and Don Nicholas Rosselli, all were very fine miniaturists who have left evidence of their worth in the splendid examples now housed at the Laurenziana, in the Nazionale and in New Saint Mary.[242] To all these we add Don Bartolomeo Della Gatta, painter and miniaturist, who was already a monk of Saint Benedict a Borgo Pinti and who later spent a few years at Holy Mary of the Angels.[243]

We should mention too, those patient monastic copyists of ancient manuscripts who served Lorenzo the Magnificent and Pope Leo X, and enriched the monastic library. There was another school at the monastery: the school of monastic weaving and embroidery. 'There are in the same Monastery of the Angels many ancient embroideries, worked with much beauty and draftsmanship by the ancient Fathers of that place.'[244]

They honored holiness and knowledge here, no less than the arts. We have already spoken of Blessed Sylvester: cook out of obedience, but wealthy with mystical gifts, a counsellor and spiritual director of souls like his—in search of God.[245] We should also mention his prior, Blessed James Geri (+1345), a monk and superior of holy life.

But the figure who stands above them all through his holiness and teaching, both sacred and humanistic, is Ambrose Traversari.[246] His name and work are identified with the monastery and Florence of his day, and he was advisor to many Florentine prelates, leaders and teachers. Some of these requested that the learned prior open an Academy next to the monastery where they could more conveniently listen to him and take advantage of his vast store of knowledge. Frequent pupils at the new Academy were: Cosimo and Lorenzo De' Medici, the Alberti, the Pucci, Coluccio Salutati, Gabriello Landini, Gino Capponi, the Albizi, the Strozzi, the Corbinelli and others.[247]

In 1379, the famous jurist Jerome Nicola Lapi became a monk there. Around 1400, Dominic Scarano, a native Greek humanist also became a monk at The Angels. He was often sought-out for explanations in his own language, then in vogue among the learned Florentines. Then there was Don Jerome, Prior Ambrose Traversari's brother, a painter, miniaturist, musician and skilled scholar. Don Sylvester Brunacci, professor of mathematics at the University of Pisa, was also a monk at The Angels. The enlightened spiritual father, Venerable Alexander Coccia died there in 1635.

The year 1348 inscribed a rather sad chapter in this luminous history. The plague which ravaged Florence in that year decimated the monks of Holy Mary of the Angels. It was necessary for some confreres to come from Camaldoli until the little group of survivors could revive. A little later, the Ciompi Uprising caused many Florentines to hide their possessions at the monastery. When the rioters heard of it, they attacked and plundered the monastery at night, killing the prior and two other monks. They even tried to set fire to the whole complex, but their attempt failed.

In 1390, Holy Mary of the Angels received autonomy from Camaldoli, with the right to elect their own prior, although still submitting the election results to the Prior General for approval.

A new era opened up for the eminent monastery in 1585 which, it must be said, damaged and changed the unique tradition and shape of the Camaldolese community. Less than three centuries after its foundation, the strict cloister was abolished and the monks were no longer 'recluses.' Consequently, the ancient claustral austerity was also mitigated.

1788 signalled the beginning of a less prosperous period. The Tuscan government cut off the Tuscan Camaldolese province from the rest of the Congregation, expelling all non-Tuscan monks. This inauspicious action served as a warning which reached fulfillment in 1808 with the Napoleonic suppression.

Upon Napoleon's fall in 1818, the monastery reopened the doors and restored the strict observance. But this was to no avail. The finishing and unfortunately, definitive touch came in 1864, when the Italian suppression took effect. The monastery was designated a hospital and the monks were expelled. The entire patrimony of holiness, arts and sciences gathered in those walls during the course of seven centuries fell to the absurdities of religious intolerance.

In recent times, the hospital transferred to the modern complex of Careggi. One part of the monastic building was set apart for the National Association of the War Disabled, which has conducted a well-conceived restoration. The other part of the building, also restored, has been placed at the University's disposition.

seven:

Historic Events

The religious aspect is, above all, what predominates in Camaldoli's history. But fit into a precise, well delineated historical/social context, Camaldoli found itself often enough involved in the civil and cultural affairs of an extensive surrounding area. Camaldoli's influence was particularly known in Tuscany and in the extensive valley of the Casentino, but many circumstances further broadened the sphere of its influence.

From its foundation, as the centuries ran their course, Camaldoli looked after the consolidation and gradual enlargement of its buildings in the Hermitage and Monastery, until it assumed its present shape. Clearly it always paid attention to what the nature of the place allowed and circumstances suggested, never disregarding aesthetic and artistic aspects.

In 1027 (the year Romuald died), Bishop Theodald of Arezzo consecrated the church of the Hermitage, and dedicated it to the Transfiguration of Jesus on Mount Tabor. One might say Camaldoli was at the beginning of its journey when a youth arrived there from his native Florence—Saint John Gualbert, the future founder of Vallombrosa and the Vallombrosian Congregation, whose part in the story in eleventh–century monasticism should be investigated more extensively.

John de' Viscomini had already experienced the drama of his brother's murder by a rival and, in obedience to Jesus' command, his soul had opened up in unconditional pardon for the murderer, kneeling in front of him and begging mercy through the blood of the crucified Christ. He carried the suffering face of Jesus dying on the cross deeply imprinted within himself. The image was a reward Jesus had given him on that Good Friday in approval of John's action. He considered becoming a monk at Camaldoli, but his own road ran elsewhere. Abbot Andrew of Strumi, one of John's first biographers, speaks of him staying many days at Camaldoli. He indicates that Gualberti's reason for deciding to leave that monastery[248] stems from Blessed Peter Dagnino, Romuald's successor, pressing him to accept the priesthood, something John was not contemplating.

1203 was a disastrous year for Camaldoli. During the night before January 18, a fire reduced the Monastery to a pile of scrap. Deciding to rebuild in a better location,[249] the monks turned to Bishop Amadeo of Arezzo who owned the desired land. But he refused, saying that it would be better to rebuild where St. Romuald himself had originally built.

The rebuilding is thought to have taken a short enough time, since we know that Cardinal Ugolino De'Conti Segni of Anagni consecrated the church in 1220. St. Francis of Assisi would have been present, because he was a guest of the Hermitage during that time.

A second blaze flared on May 31, 1276, and destroyed everything that had been built just seventy-three years before. Though the truth is difficult to verify, an historical note comments that more than three hundred monks now found themselves forced to seek shelter in various areas of the Casentino. This information is found in a letter of Prior General Gerard II (+1290) to Pope Innocent V, quoted by the Camaldolese chroniclers: 'so more than three hundred monks and *conversi* gathered to beg... *sicque plusquam trecenti inter monachos et conversos mendicare coguntur.*'[250]

When St. Francis of Assisi was at Camaldoli in 1220, he enclosed himself with Cardinal Ugolino for perhaps several weeks. One enduring tradition locates the saintly Poverello's stay in the first cell to the left of the central walkway, while the Cardinal was in the last cell on that same walkway, still called today 'the Pope's cell.'

In the Ordo Divinorum Officorum[251] we have a beautiful liturgical document dating back to 1253, composed by Prior General Blessed Martin III (+1259). It contains an extensive collection of liturgical chants in Gregorian notation, readings, responsorials, prayers for each day of the liturgical year, and the principal feasts of the Virgin Mary and Saints. In the *Constitutions*,[252] also by Martin III, precise statutes are explicated for the revision of all the material scattered among various manuscripts into a selection and comparative rearrangement. In the *Chronicon Camalduli* (unpublished and preserved in the city library of Arezzo), Baroncini states that many of these chants were composed and transcribed by a saintly hermit of Camaldoli, Blessed Pellegrine, while still another recluse, Blessed Simon, transcribed manuscripts for the library and compiled a Breviary with some chant passages.[253]

The patronage which, in a 1382 public assembly, the Florentine Republic extended to Camaldoli deserves special mention. Camaldoli was given the two regions of Prataglia Abbey and Moggiona, along with other territories belonging to them. In 1446, the Republic exempted Camaldoli from taxation. In their turn, the Medici confirmed and renewed this pledge, which lasted until 1776, when Grand Duke Peter Leopoldo rescinded the agreement.

The fifteenth century was the one most filled with cultural undertakings, but it was also a time of plundering and oppression. In 1431 a *Collegium* for boys[254] was established in the Monastery of Camaldoli, for their instruction and possibly to guide them towards monastic life. The animator was Ambrose Traversari who realizing the long–standing need, built sufficient rooms and an elegant cloister called the Boys' Cloister (Claustrum Puerorum). In the restoration of the 1950s it was returned to its original state. Prior Ambrose entrusted responsibility for the school to Don Mariotto Allegri, a learned and holy monk whom the chroniclers describe as 'devoted to the sacred sciences and embellished with religious morals.'[255] An extensive correspondence passed between Ambrose and Mariotto, full of concern, advice and recommendations of every sort. 'I recommend to you, most beloved brother, my dear consignment of youths I have given you to educate in the ways of God and raise for the heavenly host.'[256] For his part, Don Mariotto showed himself a true pedagogue and a diligent executor of his superior's directives.

In 1453 Don Mariotto was elected Prior General and he ruled the Congregation until 1478. His name is connected with two other great enterprises besides the development of the school. On the southern side of the Monastery he built the Prior General's lodging, which can be seen today, elegant, sober and simple in its fifteenth–century outline. But what is even more admirable, Mariotto founded the *Academiae Camaldulenses* for which he provided a worthy center in the magnificent salon still called the 'Academie.' Among its cultural enterprises this is without doubt the one that stands out in this period of Camaldoli's history.

This development happened during the flourishing of humanism. Following the example of Traversari, Mariotto cultivated the friendship of learned people, particularly Tuscan humanists. During the summer months they gathered at Camaldoli to discourse on philosophy, religion, literature, morality and metaphysics. Some of the distinguished names were: Lorenzo the Magnificent, Giuliano di Piero De'Medici, Cristoforo Landino, Ranuccini, Piero and Donato Acciaiuoli, Marsilio Ficino, Marco Parenti, Canigiani and Leon Battista Alberti. The sessions gave birth to the *Quaestiones Camaldulenses,* compiled by Landino. Camaldoli's example spurred on the birth of other academies in the Casentino: the Assidui of Bibbiena; the Antei of Pratovecchio; the Novelli of Poppi.

But a clarification seems necessary here. This attention paid by monks to secular culture from the fifteenth century onwards, should not be seen as merely indulging the fashion which had one of its more peculiar expressions in humanism. It is more than a matter of style. All the humanistic research and disquisition kindled a love for knowledge and study. In restoring classical humanism to the realm of the sacred, the study of the sacred sciences was considerably deepened. Schools geared towards the formation of generations of learned monks flourished in every age, and some schools became renowned.

Over the centuries, Camaldolese legislation encouraged formal studies. Don Bonaventure da Fano (+1348) who ruled the Congregation for thirty–three years is prominent in this regard. In the 1338 General Chapter at Faenza, Bonaventure promoted a wise and broad program of studies,[257] establishing schools where a solid scientific formation with special attention given to the theological/biblical disciplines, would be assured the young monks. The monasteries were gathered into nine 'federations' and one monastery from each was chosen as the central studentate. The teaching body was found among the monks of each federation. The Acts of this Chapter report these monasteries selected: St. Mary of the Vangadizza (Rovigo); St. Appollinare in Classe (Ravenna); St. Mary of Urano (Bertinoro); St. Zeno of Pisa; St. Michael in Borgo of Pisa; Holy Savior of the Berardenga (Siena); Camaldoli of Florence; St. Justus (Volterra); and St. Matthias of Murano (Venice).

A special commission of abbots and priors was also named at the Chapter, charged with drafting a special Statute, or *Ratio studiorum* for the development of studies. We have already seen that there were schools at Holy Mary of the Angels and St. Michael of Murano which, while taking care of the theological, literary and artistic formation of the young monks, were also open to the public—particularly the local nobility. Chairs at various universities, especially those of Bologna and Pisa, were awarded to various Camaldolese monks.

In 1458 an hydraulic sawmill was constructed in the immediate vicinity of the Monastery of Camaldoli for cutting lumber. It was renovated and developed in 1845 and 1879 by the mechanic John Holliger d'Argow and the monk Gabriel Dei. It functioned until 1945 and is now used as a workshop where, on the inside, a stone commemorating its last reconstruction can be seen.

The good will and protection assured Camaldoli by the Florentine Republic has been generally appreciated and reciprocated by the monks. Still there were occasions this mutual loyalty became risky and seriously damaging to Camaldoli, and the Monastery found itself paying a dear price for its faithfulness in 1498, perhaps more than at any other time.

A war between Pisa and Florence which had gone on for several months, induced the Lord of Venice to go to the aid of Pisa, since she was Venice's sister seaside republic. By autumn, the Casentino valley was infiltrated by Venetian soldiers under Carlo Orsini. Bibbiena was already in their hands. It became clear that the Venetians planned to wear down the Florentines by subduing their territory until they sued for peace. The fear grew that Camaldoli would suffer the consequences and the Prior General's Vicar, Don Basil Nardi, warned his superior who was then at St. Christina of Bologna, that he had better rush home.

Peter Delfino was Prior General, a patrician from Venice who had ruled the Congregation for eighteen years.[258] He set out immediately and arrived at Camaldoli on November 1, the Feast of All Saints. He found the monastery completely filled by people fleeing their castles, which had been seized by the enemy: men women and children in need of protection. Everyone hoped that the Prior General's Venetian background would providentially prevent Camaldoli from becoming a battlefield.

Delfino began negotiations with the Venetians at once. They had already seized some Camaldolese properties: The Mausolea, fifteen farmhouses, the little hospital at Soci, and the hospital at Bibbiena. The Prior General intended to accept no military help from the Florentines, even if they held themselves responsible, through a former pact, to defend the monastery during wartime. Delfino well understood that it would not be right to lose the pacts with the Florentines, but he also saw that Florentine intervention now would prove disastrous for the monks, the refugees and the monastery itself. Several days of dispatches passed in an attempt to find a settlement with the Venetians, but one night, as the monks were at Matins, a hundred Florentine soldiers arrived, determined to defend the monastery. The Prior General could not oppose them and had to open the doors, though he foresaw the worst.

On hearing this, the Venetians began to mistreat the few monks at the Mausolea, and swore that they would put Camaldoli to fire and sword. The news that Delfino had sided with the Florentines reached Venice, whereupon a diplomatic mission departed for Florence. The mission included Duke Guidobaldo of Urbino and Piero De'Medici. They were hoping to convince the Florentine Republic to reinstate the exiled De'Medici Lordship in their city. Once they arrived at Bibbiena and joined the Venetians there, the siege of Camaldoli seemed inevitable. On November 12, Delfino, desperate to avoid a clash, decided to rush immediately to Florence.

At dusk, a few hours after Delfino's departure, it began to snow heavily and continued through the night. The monks thought this would impede the army of four thousand ranged against them. But the Venetians were in sight of the monastery by dawn. The Florentine garrison with the monks and the refugees barricaded the entrances and took up positions at the most exposed buildings. The Duke of Urbino made a final request for the expulsion of the soldiers, but in the absence of the Prior General, the Vicar Nardi felt it outside his competence to negotiate. He took the opportunity to state that the monks had provoked no-one. He was unyielding.

Despite the rough ground and the heavy snow, the monastery was surrounded in the twinkling of an eye. Urged and helped by the monks, the Florentines had recourse to an array of weaponry: roof tiles, stones, beams, boiling water. The fighting lasted all day. The Duke of Urbino was wounded and had to abandon the field. That evening, in humiliation, the Venetians sounded the retreat, and withdrew to Casentino, leaving about forty dead and wounded on the ground. The monks immediately began to treat the wounded, and returned in the morning to bury the dead in the cloister.

There was no invasion or looting of Camaldoli, but the buildings were seriously damaged. The defeat of the Venetians caused astonishment everywhere. No one could understand how a band of at most two hundred soldiers, monks and refugees had been able to withstand a much larger force.[259]

Between 1509 and 1524, the worst damage to the buildings was repaired, and Prior General Delfino began a nearly complete reconstruction of the Monastery church. As Vasari informs us,[260] by 1361 the church had been embellished with paintings by Spinello Aretino, but all traces of this decoration have unfortunately vanished. On the basis of the design prepared by Delfino, the church took on Renaissance lines, with a panelled ceiling partially illuminated in gold, and a great arch in clear stone on the back wall, beyond which opened up a square apse with the choir and the altar at the center. Ten panels of various sizes by Giorgio Vasari and Stefano da Monte San Savino are still extant. All in all, as Delfino had wished, the church was beautiful, and the design remained until 1772, when it was recast by Mannaioni of Florence.

There was also a printshop at Camaldoli which functioned at least from 1520. It was used almost exclusively for internal work. The *Regula vitae eremiticae* and other historical/spiritual Camaldolese sources were printed there, edited by Blessed Paul Giustiniani.

Something beautiful, which is still admired today, is the Ancient Pharmacy ('Antica Farmacia') with its splendid carved cabinets and original glass and ceramics bearing the Order's coat of arms. Adjoining the pharmacy is the old galenic laboratory which served for centuries in the preparation of the medicines for which the monks were famous. A document dated May, 1048,[261] mentions a hospital at Camaldoli which gave shelter to pilgrims, cured the sick, and took care of the poor, conforming to what St. Romuald had established and Bl. Rudolf had organized. Left destroyed by the fire of 1276, the hospital could only be reopened in 1331, under Prior General Bonaventure da Fano. Another fire in 1504 prompted the hospital's move to the north of the Monastery, where it was connected to the present pharmacy. By 1543, everything had returned to normal.[262]

Now to an event of particular importance in Camaldolese history. In 1569, the ancient and renowned Hermitage of Fonte Avellana united itself with Camaldoli, along with the Congregation it headed. Fonte Avellana has already been mentioned several times as having the same tradition and characteristics analogous to Camaldoli. To outline the thousand years of history and development of this hermitage, clinging to the rock of Mount Catria, is a difficult task, rich, eventful and often determinant as it is.

Fonte Avellana was a hermitage from its origin until 1325, and then an autonomous cenobium, until Pope Paul V joined it to Camaldoli with his Bull *Quantum animus noster* on December 10, 1569.[263] It is true that this union marked the end of the Avellanita Congregation, but we can suppose that it revitalized Fonte Avellana as it did Camaldoli. What had appeared as kinship between the two houses became fraternity.

Some historians hold the year of Fonte Avellana's foundation to be 980, but 1000 seems more likely, though there are no indisputable sources.[264] We are not even sure of its founder. Various historians hold that he was a certain Bishop Ludolf of Gubbio, but there is much evidence that St. Romuald was the actual founder. While not moving beyond opinion regarding Ludolf, we certainly know the 'considerable influence, direct or indirect,'[265] exerted by the great reformer and organizer of the eremitical life: Romuald. We have already seen this in areas close to Fonte Avellana, such as Sitria, Mount Petrano and St. Vincent al Furlo.[266]

From then onwards, there was an identity between the Avellanita eremitical customs as St. Peter Damian found them and those which were in use at Camaldoli, as well as in other Romualdian places. Peter Damian's *Regula vitae eremitica* has many elements in common with the *Constitutiones* of Prior Blessed Rudolf IV of Camaldoli, particularly doctrinal elements. This supports the hypothesis for a common origin in Abbot St. Romuald.

But St. Peter Damian was the one who gave the little hermitage of Catria its determinant thrust, (details are given in Chapter 4). The Avellanita Congregation comes to birth under Peter Damian. He was its legislator and its most effective promoter, so much so that his Congregation came to include over thirty hermitages, monasteries and dependent houses in Umbria, Marche, Romagna and Abruzzo. In an even more critical way, Peter Damian was the master and father of a fervent community of true servants of the Lord, some of whom are inscribed in the register of saints.

The great service Fonte Avellana rendered the Church throughout the centuries is clearly documented, from Peter Damian's indefatigable work, to the fifty or so bishops who had lived there 'content with the contemplative life,' as Dante himself recognized. Equally relevant is the Avellanita contribution to culture through its scholars and impressive array of miniaturists, copyists and transcribers of manuscripts. The magnificent hall of the still extant scriptorium witnesses to the patient, silent labors of Avellaniti who handed down much ancient knowledge to modern times. For example, there is the *Collectio Avellana* of Bishop Corvino, later Pope Marcellus II, who researched meticulously among the manuscripts and codices of Fonte Avellana, compiling this collection of juridical norms which can stand honorably next to the *Decretum Gratiani*. A very old and consistent tradition (which I wish we could support by clearer documentation) had Dante Alighieri as a guest at Fonte Avellana in 1320. In the monastery's farthest north wing, one can still see 'Dante's room' as it has been from time immemorial.[267]

In 1392 Fonte Avellana was also subjected to the custom of a *commendam* abbot, the first being Cardinal Mezzavacca of Bologna. Commendam abbots generally do not find much sympathy, nor have they maintained a good name, particularly in monastic history. Bestowing the goods and benefices of a monastery or abbey on an outsider in deference to his civil or ecclesiastical standing, when the only purpose was to increase his fortune, must be considered a scourge. It is one of those disgraces accompanying the moral and material decadence of many monastic centers. Since Fonte Avellana remained under a commendam until the end of the eighteenth century, it could only suffer deeply. The strain of this decadence, though gradual was inexorable. Under these circumstances, Fonte Avellana met the Napoleonic and later the Italian suppressions. These suppressions were the last straw for the Fonte Avellana, as they were for Camaldoli.

Returned to the monks and restored to the Camaldolese Order after the end of the demagogic laws of suppression, Fonte Avellana today has recovered the austere beauty of its structures which arose from the tenth to the eighteenth centuries. Three contemporary priors have devoted much love and sacrifice to the complete renewal of an exceptional monastery.[268]

During the years 1980–1982, Fonte Avellana celebrated its millennium. Religious and cultural celebrations concluded with a pastoral visit by Pope John Paul II, who said:

> As I have come to speak at this fountain of spirituality, I recall in this atmosphere how everything is geared towards the values of the Spirit. God speaks to humanity's heart here where silence reigns and peace dominates... it is marvelous to think about the more than a millennium's praises which have ascended to God uninterruptedly from this monastery in the work of generations of monks... I have come today to Fonte Avellana to honor the witness and contribution which monastic life renders the Church and the world...269

In conclusion, we note here the greeting which the Pontiff gave the monastic community in private audience:

> My wish for Fonte Avellana is that it may recover a new and fervent thrust to be a center of formation and spirituality; a beacon of faith and certitude; a simple, hospitable house for those wanting to encounter Christ and climb the summits of truth and grace.[270]

St. Charles Borromeo stayed at the Hermitage of Camaldoli in 1579. The holy archbishop of Milan stayed in the newest cell of the Hermitage, built five years before by Cardinal Julius della Rovere, bishop of Urbino, and dedicated to St. Mary of Loreto. During recent times, Cardinal Ildefonse Schuster followed the example of his great predecessor.

A sizeable fire broke out in the Hermitage church on Christmas night, 1693. The last panel painted by Georgio Vasari in 1572 (representing the Coronation of the Virgin) was lost, along with the candelabra and silver plate which were melted in the conflagration. The entire building suffered damage to the extent that its upper sections became precarious. Repairs began that same year, and essential sections were completed in the following year.

Finding themselves now in the seventeenth century, the Baroque period, even the good hermits let themselves get carried away by fashion, and gave the church its current arrangement and look. The frescoes on the walls and vault, however, are quite fine. These were painted by the seventeenth–century Roman painters, Franchi and Drago, and by Passignamo, Hannibal Carracci's master.

We should add that eight hermits of Camaldoli became bishops and one was created cardinal. No one ever came and lived up here in order to escape from people, nor to wash his hands of everything involved in Church life. The monk, the hermit, and even the recluse need to continue living with the Mystical Body of Christ, if they want the blood of Christ's sap to put them forth as green and vital shoots.

Camaldoli's historical journey is not all written here, nor does it end here! Both pleasant and unpleasant parts of the journey have been mentioned, and they deserve to be told. The following pages will help Camaldoli be better known. We need to take a few steps backwards, but we will also find the road down to our own times.

eight:

Beneficial Activity:
Hospitality, Charity, Forestry

W e need to fulfil the duty of hospitality as well as possible at Fonte Bono...[271] This house was, in fact, built mainly for the purpose of hospitality. Though it would be geared cenobitically to accommodate the growing number of monks over the years, hospitality was never discontinued. Indeed nothing can be more welcome to hermits and more acceptable among the works of mercy than for the Hermitage itself to welcome all guests, particularly the poor. This hospitality must be extended with all due honor, as the Apostle says: *Practice hospitality...and do not neglect to do good and share with others what you have...*(Heb.13.2, 16). Some in the past have been rendered acceptable to the Angels through their hospitality. Christ himself is welcomed in the poor person,[272] as he himself said: *What you do to these, my little ones, you do to me* (Mt. 25.40).[273] That is how Prior Blessed Rudolf IV of Camaldoli expressed it in his Constitutions of 1080, just sixty years after the foundation.

As we see, such attention was paid to the duty of hospitality in the Benedictine tradition that the proper space was accorded hospitality in the earliest documented Camaldolese legislation. Rudolf's recommendations do not lose their validity and authority, even if that is suggested by his preoccupation with the quiet of the Hermitage not suffering from the work of hospitality. Moving beyond a simple organizational prescription, Bl. Rudolf wanted to furnish the theological/spiritual motivations of a praxis for which there are many clear examples in Sacred Scripture:

> The ministers there below (*i.e.* at the Monastery), are therefore to be busy with Martha in the constant affairs of extending holy hospitality; but their brothers (*i.e.* at the Hermitage) should sit with Mary at the Lord's feet, in their pursuit of holy contemplation. Down there let Leah bear the holy fruits of her fertility in administrational cares; here, Rachel keeps the shining eyes of her grace through contemplation of eternal light.[274]

In tune with this tradition, Camaldoli also perceived in hospitality plenty of potential for practising love's precept toward pilgrims, the poor and the sick. As time passed, Camaldolese legislation concerning hospitality was further enriched by instructions about caring for the poor and the sick. There are passages to confirm this in Bl. Martin III's *Constitutiones Camaldulenses*[275] and Bl. Gerard I's[276] *Book IV de Moribus,* where the concern that hospitality move beyond supplying food and shelter clearly emerges. The legislative instructions provide a proper foundation for organizing thoroughgoing aid and charity.

We have already mentioned that document of 1048 which refers to a hospital at Camaldoli, entrusted to a skilled monk: 'by this time there is no monastery which, following the Rule of Holy Father Benedict, would not have a hospital for welcoming the poor and curing the sick.'[277] But we should add that, besides their own hospital at Camaldoli, the monks of Camaldoli also took care of the small hospitals at Soci, Banzena and Arcena in the Casentino, along with one at Luco in Mugello. This kind of hospital work distinguished the Camaldolese almost everywhere. From a listing (which we do not claim to be complete), we can count forty-two hospitals and hospices in various parts of Italy between 1048 and 1445.[278] As we said, the rules were explicit and detailed. This can be seen in Prior General Martin III's prescription in his *Constitutiones,* Book Three, chapter thirty-four:

> To admit the poor with a smile and decorum pleasing to God and people, we strongly order each superior of our Order

take care to provide his monastery's hospital with beds and other equipment so that the poor and guests who arrive can be welcomed... We also order each superior visit the hospice of the poor and furnish what they need according to his means, so that he can manifest himself not just as a listener, but also a doer of the Gospel precept: *I was sick and you visited me*, etc.[279]

Also, in Book One, chapters thirteen and fourteen, Martin says that the infirmarian should be available to the sick 'like Christ.'[280]

There is a similar concern about charity. One particular Camaldoli custom, for example, was to choose responsible people from the neighboring towns, parish priests for the most part, who would distribute designated monies, articles of clothing or lumber to needy families, depending on their circumstances. Sometimes the community would commit itself to providing the necessary dowries for girls close to marriage. During the famines which struck the Casentino population in 1783 and 1789, the sacred vessels of the altar were pawned and the monks contracted debts of two or three thousand scudi![281]

Further afield, we see that in Florence, for example, a street of the populous St. Frediano section is still named Camaldoli today. The Camaldolese monks of Holy Savior contributed a little at a time in land and construction and built the street. Some of the houses they built are still to be seen on St. John Street, St. Leo Street, dell'Orto Street and Camaldoli Street. The Camaldolese of St. Benedict outside Porta Pinti took a similar initiative, and homes still stand bearing the Camaldolese coat of arms in Borgo Pinti, as well as along dei Tintori Street.[282]

One Camaldolese monk is particularly distinguished in his love and care of the poor, especially of the smallest ones among them—the abandoned babies, the 'little found ones' as they called them then. This monk is Bl. Dominic Vernagalli. History has not been generous with him, what has come down to us is really a small matter, but it is enough to portray this man of God in the light of authentic charity.

He was probably born at Pisa around 1180. He entered the Camaldolese house of St. Michael in Borgo in 1203. He was already a priest, and lived in the capacity as a Regular Oblate. He opened a house for abandoned children in Pisa, providing them shelter, sustenance and education. This providential hospice was built next to the monastery which fell under the direction of the abbot and Prior General of Camaldoli. Bl. Dominic died young on April 20, 1218. He had a liturgical following almost at once, which was confirmed by Pope Pius IX in 1854.

A great painting by Gandolfi in the Primaziale of Pisa, on the left as you enter, depicts the holy man founding the hospice. A beautiful text by Saint Peter Damian, himself one of the 'little found ones,' is an appropriate comment:

> When we help the needy, we do works both of mercy and truth: 'mercy' because we piously sympathize with the poor; 'truth' because we administer to them things which are theirs, not ours.[283]

•

Ecology is not our era's style. There is hardly an invention we moderns do not press to our advantage. At most, the beauty of contemporary ecology is that it announces a rediscovered love for creation. Loving the creature goes straight to the love of God. If, through this love, humanity learns to respect God and God's works, then we are right to speak of our admiration for St. Francis who, when rejoicing ecstatically in his 'Most High, Omnipotent Lord,' called the creatures together so that, together with him, they blessed the Creator: *Praise and bless the Lord; give thanks to him and serve him with great humility.*

Whoever goes up to Camaldoli today cannot escape a profound sense of wonder before the centuries–old forest which, in its majestic beauty exerts an intensely enjoyable attraction. But perhaps not all come, thinking about those who showered this vast girdle of the central Apennines with intelligent care, development and money. So we will make a brief mention of forestry and other beneficial activities promoted by the Camaldolese which, beyond being prudent, serve to integrate the facts about their care for needy people. It is true that one does not love the person without loving the environment in which that person lives.

The great forest today is Federal property of the Italian State, and it is maintained by the Forestry Corps. But before 1866, it belonged to the monks. For at least eight centuries they were the ones responsible for this patrimony, which took on its present dimensions partly through donations and partly through acquisitions. The importance placed on forestry was such that the monks quickly found themselves having to study organizational, experimental and structural standards from safeguarding the forest from uncontrolled infringements. And so was born all the wise forestry legislation, promoted and updated as circumstances required, by the General Chapters, and which ultimately became part of the Camaldolese Constitutions.

Examination of this rich documentation presents a clear idea of Camaldoli's contribution in this sphere of socio-economic development. It is sufficient for us to note some pieces of this legislation. For more information see the study of Don Joseph Cacciamani.[284]

> The fathers of the Hermitage should take the greatest care and diligence that the woods and fir trees not be diminished in any way, but rather spread out and increased with new plantings, the protection of hedges, the watchfulness of custodians who drive away livestock, without letting expenditure for that end decide matters. And let whoever looks after all this be diligent in his office. When some trees must be cut down, he should make sure he is present so those fir trees are cut in areas where the woods will not be diminished and take away from its beauty and charm... Beyond this, let the superiors make sure that somehow four or five thousand fir trees get planted each year.[285]

The monks were more than faithful to these prescriptions, and the number of trees planted in 1857 and 1859, for example, surpassed those already established—by ten thousand and thirty thousand respectively—and this on the eve of the forest's nationalization! It appears there were two main concerns in the management of the forest: to thin the trees in a way that would not change the forest mantle; and to respect its beauty by never cutting along the main roads. 'And some trees should always be left along the main road for ornamentation and shade.'[286]

With such wise standards and centuries of experience, the Camaldolese monks became true ecological cultivators. To all others, they were masters in taking care of the forest, as well as deriving the greatest possible profit from it. They showed clearly enough that art often knows well how to adjust nature at the right moment and regain the advantage right there, where it had seemed less favorable.[287]

As in the forest sector, the agriculture also enjoyed the benefits of such education. Vast areas around Arezzo were reclaimed, along with parts of Valdarno, Val di Chiana, Maremma and the neighborhood of Borgo San Sepolchro: all owing much to the monks' skilfulness. When the Forest of Camaldoli became Federal property in 1866, it covered one thousand four hundred and forty–two hectares (three and a half million acres). Through successive acquisitions for the Italian Forestry Corps work, the forest today covers an additional three hundred and twenty–one hectares (about eight hundred thousand acres).

nine:

Dissensions and Suppressions

The image of a wisely articulated pluralism which guarantees a variety of choices within the harmony of one monastic profession, is certainly one which has emerged from all we have noted thusfar.

The Camaldolese institution with all its various components—cenobium and hermitage, reclusion and apostolate—has always enabled each person's character and balance to develop harmoniously. These are the conditions which allow a free and responsible answer to the call of the Holy Spirit. The primary value for the Congregation's progressive evolution is unity, and this is threatened if one flawed component of Camaldolese life is disproportionately addressed. It is a problem which often surfaces in capitular dispositions or in the visits and actions of Priors General.

Surely it is providential that Camaldoli—Monastery and Hermitage—could have eluded the scourge of the *commendam*, which as we know condemned many famous Italian monastic centers to wither away and die. But symptoms of real and progressive malaise were not lacking in Camaldoli's thousand–year history. The symptoms grew into internal crises which set the stage for very real divisions. Unity was sacrificed more out of misunderstanding than as a result of principle.

This is not the place for analyzing the causes of separation, nor to make any judgment. These notes are limited to events in their evolution and realization, certainly deeply regretted, which five centuries of tradition should have helped in enlightening minds and avoiding the suffering resulting from disunity.

The first indications of a tendency toward autonomy from Camaldoli as *caput et mater* (head and mother) began to appear at St. Michael of Murano, presumably encouraged by pressures from other Venetian communities. A privilege dating to Pope Gregory XII (1407) which had granted the monks of Murano the right to elect their abbot without the customary submission of election results for the Prior General's approval, was perhaps the remote cause, even if it was not realized at the time. Gradually it nourished the mentality that yearned for independence.

We know sometimes how particular situations reach completion: lacking any 'real' indications or elements—as the present case seems to be—they create 'pretextual' ones. Of course, without wishing it so, vanity itself can be enough to make a spirit of emulation grow!

During the fifteenth and sixteenth centuries, it was already known in the Order that there was a general need for reorganization. We should recognize that there was no lack of incentive, even from the Holy See itself. Perhaps a reform like Louis Barbo's new Benedictine reform at Saint Justina of Padua was considered, but the idea found no consensus.

So the monks arrived at the 1446 General Chapter at St. Savino of Pisa, presided by Prior General Francis D'Agna. Setting aside the 'St. Justina' project, the capitulars searched for something analogous which would not force them to battle centuries–old tradition, and yet would open the way toward reorganization. Many were now expecting it. A compromise was reached: the Congregation was divided into nine groups, each with a 'head' monastery to which the other monasteries in the group referred. The Chapter reduced controls on various specific matters, while giving the impression that every attempt at division would be exorcized. Such was not the case.

The problem reappeared in all its guises in the 1474 Chapter at Fonte Bono, presided by Prior General Mariotto. A discreet number of capitulars conceived the possibility of a new arrangement: one congregation composed of St. Michael of Murano, St. Matthais and St. Mary delle Carceri; and a second congregation composed of Camaldoli, Holy Mary of the Angels and St. Benedict in Florence. No formal decisions were made, true, but the idea gained ground at the theoretical level. The Chapter closed and everyone returned home.

A little later, something more decisive came from Murano. That same Chapter year, Abbot Peter Donato who had returned to St. Michael of Murano, made the first tentative contacts with the government of the Venetian Republic. He wanted to erect an autonomous congregation of the Venetian monasteries, with St. Michael of Murano at the helm. Negotiations ensued, and the Council of Ten reacted favorably. At the time, the Holy See needed to win favor with the Venetians, so it confirmed the project. The 'cenobitical' Congregation of St. Michael of Murano was born, at least on paper.

Matters coincided to made it fact. That famous privilege of 1407 from Pope Gregory XII was confirmed by Pope Sixtus IV in 1474, precluding any intervention by Camaldoli. Indeed, powerless against the Holy See's authority, Prior General Mariotto Allegri, could only resort to moral persuasion, to try to convince Murano to draw back from damaging Camaldolese unity. He received fleeting promises. Don Mariotto died soon afterwards, on September 28, 1478. His successor, Don Jerome Grifoni died after only two years as Prior General.

Don Peter Delfino, the new abbot of St. Michael of Murano was present at the 1480 General Chapter for the election of a new Prior General. It seemed to signify that the bridges with Camaldoli were not yet entirely broken. The largest bloc of votes deferred to Delfino so the capitulars elected him Prior General, hoping that a professed monk of Murano as Prior General could prevent the final break.

Unfortunately, these hopes proved ungrounded. The entire Order, particularly Camaldoli itself, was aware that new ideas had taken hold on the slippery ground of internal disputes, and were slowly penetrating minds and surroundings. And even though the ideas were not rooted in legislation, the Murano monks were to all intents and purposes independent of Camaldoli. They continued to compromise, though discord rather than agreement was the order of the day.

Pope Innocent VIII, who had been approached by the monks of Murano, intervened in 1488, adding to the privileges that had been granted by his predecessors. This served to reinforce Murano's autonomy. They announced a *Consulta* of all the superiors of the Venetian monasteries, but without the Prior General! New, special 'rules' were laid down. Substantially this was a General Chapter in perfect form. From this point the opposition between Murano and Camaldoli was out in the open.

Meanwhile the Venetian Paul Gustiniani, a good friend of Delfino, entered the Camaldoli Hermitage as a postulant in December, 1510, at the age of thirty–four. He had degrees in philosophy and theology from the University of Padua—a man of vast culture and extraordinary gifts of the Spirit. Delfino welcomed him as a gift from God, so great were his esteem and hopes in the new arrival. Giustiniani's mature age and proven virtue induced the Prior General to request a special indult from the Apostolic See so he could enter the Hermitage at once, dispensing with the ordinary practice of first proving himself in the Monastery. In January, 1511, he was joined by two of his old friends, Vincent Peter Quirini and Sebastian Giorgi who, in their turn were clothed in the Camaldolese habit. All three professed vows on August 8, 1512.

Through Quirini, who had been ambassador of Venice to Emperor Maximilian and the King of Spain, Giustiniani was introduced in high ecclesiastical and civil circles. Now in Tuscany, they had the opportunity to meet Cardinal John De'Medici, the Pontifical Legate for the Florentine Republic. A little later Giustiniani would get great support from these acquaintances.

A few years were sufficient for Giustiniani to become well aware of the quarrels and disharmony disturbing the regular observance at the Hermitage and Monastery. Many complaints which the sound and well–intentioned part of the community brought before Delfino came to nothing. The Prior General, recognized as virtuous and truly monastic, was strangely unable to believe the complaints. By nature he was reluctant to think that some of his confreres, whether hermits or cenobites, might not act in good faith.

There were conflicting habits of discipline, administrative gaps, habitual absence of some hermits from the Hermitage, all contributing to widespread discontent. The good monks sought to mitigate the problems, while restless monks stirred up things with their murmurings and advocated drastic solutions. In maintaining strict neutrality, Delfino did not realize that he was provoking some of the dissent himself. It is certain he did not grasp the need to bring about adequate reforms. He was under the illusion of thinking things would work themselves out in time.

In 1513, Giustiniani found himself at the center of this disquiet. He took to heart the frequent claims and pressures of the brethren, and believed that reform could not be delayed any longer. Consulting Quirini and the holy recluse Don Michael, and with the support of Cardinal John De'Medici, he obtained permission from Pope Julius II to induce Delfino to convoke an extraordinary General Chapter. The date was set for the day after Easter, 1513. On the agenda were: consideration of reuniting the two congregations, a courageous and timely reform and— something new for Camaldoli—the abolition of lifetime Priors General. This latter was the result of the growing conviction that at least part of the current uneasiness sprang from Delfino as an individual or his office running too long.

Giustiniani and Quirini prepared the agenda carefully. The Monastery of Holy Mary of the Angels in Florence was chosen as the venue. Pope Julius II had died on March 9, 1513, and Cardinal De'Medici succeeded him, taking the name Leo X. Given his friendship with Giustiniani and

Quirini, the possibilities for supporting the message of the two Venetians began to take root in many monks.

The Chapter opened in April. The discussions were animated and controversial, but without too much trouble. The opinion that the Chapter should agree with the two hermit's proposals soon prevailed. So they managed to reconstruct the Congregation's unity, albeit by compromise.

A new name was given to the Camaldolese union: The Camaldolese Congregation of the Holy Hermitage and St. Michael of Murano. This palliative sought to appease both sides, which had been pretending for some decades to recognize each other. But the palliative concealed a deception. The equation carried uncertainties. The least one could say is that actually, the two congregations treated each other as equals, and the former link with Camaldoli had had its day. The announced reform would cut a wide swathe. Meticulous and far–reaching, it involved everything and spared no one, high and low alike. It aimed at a return to the spirit of the primitive Order. Lastly, the capitulars decided to abolish the centuries–old custom of lifetime Priors General. They would be henceforth replaced at a given interval, ordinarily every three years. The Chapter closed at the end of the month.

The Congregation still needed the Apostolic See's ratification. This was entrusted to Giustiniani and Quirini, who left for Rome on May 10. They did not have to wait long. Pope Leo X issued the Bull *Esti a summo*[289] on July 7, approving the Chapter Acts. Prior General Peter Delfino immediately left office after ruling the Order for thirty–three years. He did not fail to make his protest, trusting in his old friendship with the Pontiff, but its outcome was insignificant and the well known *pro bono pacis* (for the good of peace) prevailed. Delfino left Camaldoli and returned to his own monastery of Murano, where he died on January 15, 1525.

Many Camaldolese appeared convinced that the final word had been said. The Papal Bull seemed to represent the 'providential moment.' But this was not the case. The rediscovered unity, new internal organization, the triennial election of local and General superiors, the confirmation of the traditional procedure regulating relations between hermitage and monastery (Camaldoli was the major representative): all promised a new era of vitality. This was more polite illusion than real conviction.

Giustiniani himself, perhaps for the first time, had to acknowledge that restoring harmony was not the same as organizing a Chapter! The Hermitage, which had been foremost in his efforts continued to present serious 'personal' problems. Eremitical observance was well below the ideal. Don Paul yearned for a more austere lifestyle, stricter silence and solitude, and he believed that elements of the solitary life were simply insufficiently appreciated at Camaldoli. His uneasiness stemmed from the interlacing of material cares and frequent gossiping which engaged him as superior. And so his proposal to reform the eremitical life re–emerged. He prayed and pondered much. Through Quirini, he sought counsel from the Pope, who received him and listened to him. Convinced of Giustiniani's good intentions, Leo X could only encourage him in his various attempts. A little later, in 1520, he approved Giustiniani's *Regula vitae eremiticae* and consented that he should test it in founding new hermitages.

Don Paul was greatly encouraged by this and on September 14, 1520, left Camaldoli and retired with some companions to the caves of Massaccio near Cupramontana which had been given them by the monks of Camaldoli. Here he practically gave rise to a new, exclusively eremitical congregation, which he named the Company of Hermits of St. Romuald.

It is unlikely that Giustiniani intended to split with Camaldoli. What was probably in his heart was a greater autonomy and to try with his little band, to live the former eremitical ideal. His confreres at Camaldoli probably did not understand well enough what he proposed, and saw in his departure the beginning of division. Friction between the groups grew until the Company celebrated its own first

General Chapter in 1526, where for all practical purposes the rupture of all juridical connections with Camaldoli was sanctioned.

The new 'congregation' developed well. Within a century it was firmly established in Italy and had a good number of hermitages in Poland. The first name was dropped and replaced with 'The Congregation of Camaldolese Hermits of Monte Corona,' named for the splendid hermitage near Umbertide in Umbria. This is their name today. Men outstanding in holiness and austerity of life thronged to the hermitages of the new congregation, which reached its peak of growth during the seventeenth century.

Don Paul Giustiniani died a holy death at Mount Soratte on June 28, 1528, at the age of fifty–two. Don Gregory da Bergamo, the Elder Father of Camaldoli at the time, rushed to assist him. He left writings on Sacred Scripture and in Apologetical and Mystical Theology, with more than two hundred completed manuscripts and a hundred incomplete. A particular merit stems from him being one of the first voices calling for the introduction of the vernacular into the liturgy.[290]

What about the relations between Murano and Camaldoli? The differences had not decreased. In fact, we should say any excuse seemed good for deepening the reciprocal incompatibility. Further, the success of Giustiniani's reform also encouraged the cenobites to cut themselves off from Camaldoli, formally and definitively in 1616.

Within a century, the age–old Camaldolese trunk found itself divided into three branches. Scant comfort of having left the 'name' to the two offshoots remained for Camaldoli.

The cenobitical Congregation of Murano also experienced its own beautiful flowering. Many famous saints, scholars and monks awarded the highest Church offices, came out of her monasteries. The Congregation existed until July 5, 1935, when Pope Pius XI's *Inter Religiosos coetus* reunited her with Camaldoli.

Given the purely informative nature of this work, we do not seek to evaluate or judge this succession of events. But it is certainly legitimate to express deep regret. After all, the Camaldolese union has paid the heaviest price. A perceptive theologian and good friend of Camaldoli has written:

> Romuald's disciples later considered breaking this integral program of contemplation and apostolate into pieces, but the secret of their rebirth remains in that integrality and the intelligent, authentic return to those sources.[291]

But the hard times were not yet completely over. Clouds of another massive storm were gathering in the skies of history: the suppression of all the religious orders in Italy. Neither Camaldoli nor the other two congregations sharing it name, escaped this new downpour. Here is not the place to search for the remote causes of this fury which various European states hurled at their ecclesiastical institutions. As far as motivations go, we should not really go beyond those of a merely political nature, which serve as an excuse. Though many can be considered, the real reason for confrontations with the Church remains intolerance, first in an underhanded fashion, but later manifested quite openly. Italy experienced two suppressions in less than sixty years.

At the time of his Italian campaign, Napoleon Bonaparte, who had seized ecclesiastical possessions in 1810, began to suppress all religious orders, confiscating their property, stealing artworks and precious objects and finally expelling the religious from their monasteries. After the French dictator's fall, the Congress of Vienna (1815) abolished the laws of suppression. The religious orders recovered those possessions which had escaped the plundering, and were allowed back into those monasteries which were not already put to another use.

The various groups made enormous efforts to begin anew, but a second suppression squelched the attempts. Under pressure from the Cavour government in 1866, King Victor Emanuele II signed a new decree of suppression similar to Napoleon's.

All the property of Camaldoli—furniture, real estate, buildings and forest—went over to the State. The monks were expelled. For the most part, the immense, precious archival patrimony ended up in the State archives in Florence. The monks were allowed to return to the Hermitage some years later, but only in the capacity of custodians! A rental fee was contracted in 1873, referring only to the residential sections and places of worship. Even today, the monks of Camaldoli are present there only under these conditions.

ten:

Camaldoli Today

Reading the past contributes to forming culture, and culture is always an integral part of a people's or an institution's soul. And so, tradition is born from that 'given,' as it were, from years and centuries of living. Tradition does not simply hark back to a fixed sequence of things which have already happened and are no longer repeatable, but points out its value as a continuous, vital part which can justify and strengthen present behavior.

So, reading the past is a good and formative thing, but even better, it revives the present, if that present can interpret it. This is a surety because it does not surrender itself to simple, mechanical repetition of how we behaved yesterday, but persists as a principle to which we can refer to derive new models for acting in harmony with the progressive evolution of history. History is not only a 'yesterday' which one reads so as not to forget, but also a 'today' which asks to be documented, lived and interpreted.

Does Camaldoli's history have a sequel? If it does, what kind of face does it show in the contemporary fabric of Church and world? In short, does Camaldoli live its 'today,' and how so?'

When the conversation turns to monasticism which, as an independent phenomenon, takes us back to the first centuries of the Christian era, the need arises to verify if monasticism today is something vital which can affect the present positively. In short, people demand, very sincerely, that monks justify their validity and usefulness. People want a monk to be one who is most attentive to the signs of his times precisely because they think he has singled out from

151

the entanglement of a thousand projects that one which is essential to existence. They want new ways of acting for new times—fresh answers. And the answers must always be coupled with the ancient tradition, but expressing the dynamism and truth of that event which is always new, the event of Jesus Christ.

It appears that the community now living at Camaldoli realizes its responsibility before such demands. This is seen in the effort it makes to discern whether it has found its own way of being a living part of the Mystical Body of Christ, committed to give humbly and seriously its response to contemporary humanity.

Half a century ago, tourism discovered this magnificent corner of the Tuscan Apennines in central Italy, making Camaldoli a stop on an excursion which included Vallombrosa and La Verna. The broad valley of the Casentino is rich in history, the arts and natural beauty. It is circumscribed, almost protected by a nearly perfect triangle: Camaldoli to the north, on the Giogana slopes; La Verna, the 'rough rock' to the east; and Vallombrosa to the west, carefully placed on the back of Pratomagno. These are three citadels of the Spirit where two monastic communities, and one Franciscan, have lived for a millennium, standing 'firm at God's service,'[292] to use Dante's expression.

This expression puts the painting in the right frame. Camaldoli is really one of these citadels, born and continuing only for the service of God and those who have taken up life there in this service. Whoever comes to Camaldoli should know that, even if he has no idea at all of becoming a monk, he will encounter God, tracing the same journey of the monk who comes to the monastery only 'to seek God.'[293]

After their first impression of the great forest which welcomes and almost enfolds one in its green mantle, many stand before these centuries-old buildings and ask themselves 'What do these monks do?' There is an answer, but it obviously is one which emerges from a faith-context, beyond which nothing makes sense in such a place. So, they take it for granted that only such a band of persons can be satisfied because, for these, the monk alone succeeds in saying something about the reality within themselves in a more natural way. The monk has discovered here his way to live and announce his faith in the Risen Lord Jesus. The value of 'Christian witness' is seen even in the monk's choice which, in whatever way or form it takes shape, proves interesting when he declares it.

The monk's position is not different from the simple Christian one, in the sense that it also finds justification in faith which, as it evolves, comes to hold God alone as the goal of everyone. This goal is where we find our own full glory and realization, not our annihilation. Faith–responses come from faith–choices; without faith's lens, monastic life appears useless.

To help formulate an answer, some compare the monk's choice to that of the missionary, parish priest, hospital sister, etc. The missionary 'serves' and 'one understands;' the monk, less so, or really not at all. All this refers to the current mentality which judges the value of human existence on its 'usefulness.' Humanity seems convinced that self–realization lies in proportion to its yield in goods.

Christian faith–experience, basically experiences of the Spirit, cannot be reduced to the measure of forming an opinion or not. They show clearly and humbly that ideals which are possible to attain, surpass human life and go far beyond contingency. Humanity is in a position to touch authentic summits whenever it succeeds in being a sign of the transcendent realities for which God created it. Whoever decide to put the search for God first, finds themselves in opposition to everything which reduces humanity solely to material considerations. Monasticism has always served as a rebuke to those who put the provisional 'idols' first. Here monasticism is 'prophetic' with a voice crying out in the desert of confusion and bewilderment, so that the pathways might be straightened.[294]

This is also the acknowledgment Vatican II expresses, seeing the monks precisely as an eschatalogical sign, characterizing the Church which lives and works in time, but is waiting to rejoin Christ, her Spouse, in the Kingdom of Heaven:

> The sacred Council appreciates very much their kind of virginal, poor and obedient life whose model is Christ, and again places its firm hope in their many works–hidden or manifest. All religious, animated by honest faith, by charity toward God and neighbor, by love for the cross and by hope in the glorious future, spread the good news of Christ throughout the world, so that their witness is clear to all, and our Heavenly Father is glorified (Mt. 5.16).[295]

The call to the primary nature of the monastic choice is of great significance—to follow Christ, virginal, poor and obedient, with whom the monk identifies his own specific calling in the Church, making manifest to all brothers and sisters throughout the world that monastic life contributes to spreading Christ's name everywhere and to serving the Gospel cause.

The idea of monastic life as an end in itself collapses. The so–called 'cloister' also rediscovers its role as a means, pure and simple, certainly useful, but far from any pretense of being radically separate. The true values to seek and defend, will be seen in the variety of gifts with which the Spirit enriches the Church and individual souls. There is such a wonderful variety of gifts which manifest *the manifold wisdom of God* (Eph, 3.10) and contribute to *the upbuilding of the Body of Christ* (Eph.4.12). What is asked of monastic community is the availability and capacity to open itself up with wisdom and prudence beyond the limits of its living environment. It is to show charity and interest in everyone, aware that its search for God does not exempt it from caring for others. In fact, it is often through others that the monk finds God.

The reflection that Camaldoli is moving forward, particularly during these post–conciliar years, is drawn from such criteria, not really new approaches for being and acting appropriately.

Monastic community makes its journey in the sense and direction indicated, aware of the precarious nature of each attempt. In order not to run *like one aimlessly* (ICor. 26.9), but with a calm, objective and sustained re–examination of tradition (the incentive for Vatican II), it has readapted some disciplinary, structural and organic norms. These 'givens' are confronted with new and urgent requests for reassessment from outside and within the monastic community.

A good, critical analysis singled out some specific characteristics of the Camaldolese institution to hold them unchanged. This was done without feeling humiliated at having to offer itself as an image of freshness, almost of modernity. Studying the past has not been easy, respecting its genuine values and not denying what is always alive there. How laborious it has been to insert that study into the new journey!

We must thoroughly respect and re–evaluate that providential, almost unique 'pluralism' of the Camaldolese monastic family, which has revealed sources of uncommon energies in the Church and western monasticism. Indeed, with its particularity of cenobitical and eremitical life, or reclusion and apostolate, the Congregation of Camaldoli today shows itself in all its variety, fully respectful of the freedom with which the Spirit draws each person.

At Camaldoli the large guesthouse has been placed at the disposition of all Christians and non–Christians, a concrete service of charity, offering the possibility of more attentive listening to the Word of God and commitment to prayer. This gives to the monastery a remarkable sense of 'feeling with the Church.'

The care and dialogue of the monastic community have broadened to embrace people of other creeds, Jews, and other non–Christian religions. Thus the monks have been able to benefit from contact with many different religious experiences, fostering ecumenism which is typical of this stage of Universal Church history.

Such encounters are articulated and vitalized by two privileged moments: Eucharist and the communal reflection on the Word of God. Eucharist, the center and foundation for growth of the monastic community, is presented as the essential moment for proclaiming common faith in the Risen Jesus and building communion with all who are Christ's. Connected to the eucharistic moment, reflection on the Word of God continues well beyond the purely liturgical celebration. Here the monk, whom the Rule has taught a sapiental reading of Scripture, has an opportunity to use his personal experience devoted to *lectio divina* in a spirit of service to his confreres. The Liturgy of the Hours, then, is a celebration in praise, song and communal adoration, in which the monks express and share that profound yearning of humanity's heart, which within the communion of the Church, is the 'spouse's voice.'

The dialogue between the confreres has been taken up and amplified for the quarterly journal *Vita Monastica*,[296] variously concerned with monastic issues, theological, ecumenical, and so on. Besides this, a smaller pamphlet *Lettere agli amici* maintains connections with the many friends of Camaldoli, keeping them informed on the significant moments of the community's journey and providing them a forum for suggestions, opinions and remarks.

This family of our friends is already large. The monks experience there a gift of the Holy Spirit through the present moment of history, and to them, particularly, we wish to dedicate these pages which hopefully will help them and others know the patrimony of faith, of the activity and Christian witness which has blossomed on the thousand year–old trunk planted in *Campo Amabile,* and watered at Fonte Bono.[297]

•

The following is a list of the hermitages and monasteries which now compose the Camaldolese Congregation in Italy and elsewhere.

156

CAMALDOLI, eleventh century, Holy Hermitage and Monastery. Diocese and Province of Arezzo, Italy. A special juridical norm forms one community from monks living in two localities. The prior, by ancient right, the reigning Prior General of the entire Congregation,[298] is the Superior. The Prior General is helped in the governing the Congregation by a Council of three Assistants, while he uses two vice–priors for governing the Holy Hermitage and the Monastery at Camaldoli. A monk's move to, or stay at, one or the other of these two environs is a matter of choice, with the prior's consent, or if there is a need to lend help to one or the other. The Hermitage is the residence of the postulants; the Monastery, of novices. Hospitality is provided by both: at the Hermitage, for small groups wanting an experience of prayer; at the Monastery, for larger groups often with specific purposes: study and reflection weeks, formative gatherings geared to theology, liturgy, biblical studies and culture.

FONTE AVELLANA, tenth century. Unified dioceses of Fano, Fossombrone, Cagli and Pergola, Province of Pesaro, Italy. Situated at the foot of Mount Catria in the Marche region, at its border with Umbria. This is a *sui juris* community, *i.e.* elects its own prior, has its own novices and professed monks. They offer hospitality to groups and individuals.

SAINTS BLASE AND ROMUALD, thirteenth century. Diocese of Fabriano, Province of Ancona, Italy. The tomb of St. Romuald is in the crypt of the church, which is also a parish church.

SAINT GREGORY AL CELIO, Camaldolese since the sixteenth century. Diocese and Province of Rome, Italy. Locality for the general studentate (the young professed monks).

CAMALDOLI OF NAPLES, Diocese and Province of Naples, Italy. This hermitage belonged to the Camaldolese Congregation of Monte Corona until 1962, when it was transferred to the Camaldolese Congregation of the Order of St. Benedict. It has the juridical status 'semi–independent' and can have its own novices and professed monks. Hospitality is offered to individuals and small groups.

HERMITAGE OF MONTE GIOVE, Diocese of Fano, Province of Pesaro, Italy. It belonged to the Camaldolese Congregation of Monte Corona until 1925, when it transferred to the Camaldolese Congregation of the Order of St. Benedict. Hospitality is offered to individuals and small groups.

SACCIDANANDA ASHRAM (Hermitage of the Trinity), Diocese of Tiruchirapali, State of Tamil Nadu, India. Founded in 1950, it has been Camaldolese since 1980.

NEW CAMALDOLI HERMITAGE, Diocese of Monterey, California, U.S.A. This hermitage was founded in 1958 and is an eremitical community *sui juris*. It extends hospitality to individuals.

INCARNATION MONASTERY, Diocese of Oakland, California, U.S.A. Founded in 1982, this urban community, dependent upon New Camaldoli, serves as a house of studies for monks. It offers hospitality to individuals.

MONASTERY OF THE TRANSFIGURATION DI MOGI DAS CRUZES, Diocese of Mogi das Cruzes, State of Sao Paulo, Brazil. Founded in 1985, this monastery offers hospitality to individuals.

EPIPHANY MONASTERY, Diocese of Manchester, New Hampshire, U.S.A. Founded in 1992, this dependent monastery of New Camaldoli offers hospitality to small groups and individuals.

HERMITAGE OF SAINT GEORGE, Diocese and Province of Verona, Italy. This formerly belonged to the Camaldolese Congregation of Monte Corona. The Camaldolese Congregation of the Order of St. Benedict took residence there in 1993, offering hospitality to small groups and individuals.

HERMITAGE OF SAINT HELEN. Diocese and Province of Treviso, Italy. This House of Prayer opened in 1979, is run by diocesan priests who are Camaldolese Oblates Regular.

Camaldolese Nuns are presently located at:

SAINT JOHN THE EVANGELIST, twelfth century, (Pratovecchio). Diocese of Fiesole; Province of Arezzo, Italy.

SAINT MAGLORIO, fourteenth century. Diocese of Faenza; Province of Ravenna, Italy.

SAINT CATHERINE, seventeenth century. Diocese of Faenza, Province of Ravenna, Italy.

SAINT ANTONY, ABBOT, eighteenth century. Diocese and Province of Rome, Italy.

SAINT JOHN THE BAPTIST, twentieth century. Diocese and Province of Arezzo, Italy.

SS. ANNUNZIATA, twentieth century. Diocese and Province of Arezzo, Italy.

IMMACULATE HEART OF MARY, twentieth century. Diocese and Section of Toulon, France.

CAMALDOLESE NUNS, twentieth century. Zloczew (Vloctavek), Poland.

CAMALDOLESE NUNS O.S.B., twentieth century, Diocese of Iringa, Tanzania.

TRANSFIGURATION MONASTERY, twentieth century. Diocese of Rochester, New York, U.S.A.

EMMAUS, twentieth century. (House of Prayer) Diocese and Province of Arezzo, Italy.

The holy Church of Christ is united
and formed with such charity, that
all together, they form a single body
and, in a mysterious way,
the whole Church is present in each.
So, the Universal Church is correctly called
the one Spouse of Christ.
Each soul is the whole Church,
through the mystery of unity...
Since the entire Church
is represented in one person
and called a single virgin,
the holy Church is simultaneously one
in all her members
and entire within each of them.
Within the plurality there is the unity of faith,
many united in each through the bond of charity
and the variety of gifts,
because all come from one.

Although the holy Church is divided into
many members, she is fused into unity by
the Holy Spirit's flame. [299]

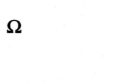

Notes and References

1. St. Peter Damian, a native of Ravenna, a hermit, Prior of Fonte Avellana, theologian, writer, Bishop and Cardinal of Ostia, was the first biographer of St. Romuald. He wrote this *Life* 15 years after Romuald's death (1042) and, though he did not know him personally, he obtained information from various disciples of the reformer. Peter Damian died at Faenza, Feb. 21, 1072. For the citations from the *Life of St. Romuald (Vita di S. Romualdo)* we will use the abbreviation **VR.** The critical edition of *Vita Beati Romualdi*, edited by Giovanni was published at Rome in 1957 by Istituto storico italiano per il Medio Evo, in the collection 'Fonti per la storia d'Italia,' vol. 94.

2. VR, Chapter 4.

3. VR, Chapter 1.

4. Ibid.

5. Ibid.

6. VR, Chapter 2.

7. VR, Chapter 3.

8. VR, Chapter 4.

9. Ibid. The *Annales Camaldulensis* (AA.CC.) situate Marino's hermitage at Tor di Caligo, east of Piave in the neighborhood of Iesolo, making Fortunio's thesis their own. Cf. A. Fortunio, *Historiarum Camaldulensium pars posterior*, Venice 1579, quoted by AA.CC., I, page.53.

10. VR, Chapter 4.

11. Ibid.

12. The monastery of St. Michael of Cuxa is situated in the Countship of Confluent, in Rossiglione, at the foot of Mount Canigou in the Eastern Pyrenees. Today a small monastic community lives there, dependent upon the Benedictine Abbey of Montserrat near Barcelona, Spain.

13. VR, Chapter 5.

14. Ibid.

15. According to Anonimo of Rivopol, author of the *Life of Bl. Peter Orseolo (Vita b. Petri Urseoli)*, a sixth companion was added, one John Mauroceno, afterwards the founder of St. George the Greater (San Giorgio Maggiore) monastery on the island of the same name at Venice. Cf. J. Mabillon, *Acta Sanctorum Ordinis Sancti Benedicti*, VII, Venice 1737, p.849. Also see AA.CC. I, pp.131,160,412.

16. VR, Chapter 6.

17. Ibid.

18. VR, Chapter 9.

19. Ibid.

20. Bruno of Querfurt, *Life of the Five Brothers and Letter to King Henry (Vita dei cinque fratelli e lettera a re Enrico)*, edited by Bernardo Ignesti, Edizioni Camaldoli, 1951, p.36. This will be referred to as **V5F**. The 'Rule' is surely Saint Benedict's Rule, either because Romuald had professed it at Classe (Ravenna) or because, until the rise of the Mendicant Orders (13th & 14th centuries), people understood the *Regula Monasterium* as either St. Benedict's or St. Augustine's.

21. VR, Chapter 12.

22. VR, Chapter 15.

23. VR, Chapter 16.

24. VR, Chapter 17.

25. Ibid.

26. VR, Chapter 18. This concerns the monastery of St. Michael near Verghereto (Forli), now defunct. Ugo of Tuscany (953–1001), son of Uberto, friend and supporter of Otto III, was his adviser for Roman and Southern Italian politics.

27. VR, Chapter 18.

28. VR, Chapter 19.

29. The Hermitage of Fonte Avellana dates back to around 980, and contemporary to Romuald, is situated at the foot of Mount Catria in the Umbrian–Marchigiano Apennines (700 m.). Venerated for its sanctity and learning, St. Peter Damian (+1072) became a monk there and later, Prior and legislator. Many other monastic saints and scholars blossomed at Fonte Avellana, 46 of whom became bishops. This Hermitage was head of the Avellanita Congregation which was incorporated into the Camaldolese Congregation by Pope Pius V in the 16th cent. The first millennial celebrations of F.A. (1980–1982) concluded with the presence of Pope John Paul II on Sept. 5th 1982.

30. Regarding recluses and reclusion, see this book's sections: 'Signs of A Presence,' and 'Four Hermit Recluses at the Hermitage of Camaldoli.'

31. VR, Chapter 20.

32. VR, Chapter 21.

33. Otto III of Saxony (980–1002). Along with Pope Sylvester II, he undertook a religious renewal of the Empire. He promoted evangelization of the pagan areas between Western Russia (Kiev) and Poland, finding active collaboration in his great friend, St. Romuald and some of his disciples.

34. VR, Chapter 22.

35. Ibid.

36. Ibid.

37. VR, Chapter 23.

38. Ibid.

39. Ibid.

40. VR, Chapter 24.

41. VR, Chapter 25.

42. Ibid.

43. Ibid.

44. Ibid.

45. VR, Chapter 26.

46. VR, Chapter 15.

47. V5F, pp.33–34, 36.

48. VR, Chapter 26.

49. Ibid.

50. Ibid.

51. V5F, Introduction, p.1.

52. VR, Chapter 27.

53. This is the basilica of the monastery of Saints Boniface and Alexis–on–the–Aventine in Rome. The titular saint is Boniface, the great apostle of Germany, bishop of Magonza and martyr of Fulda.

54. VR, Chapter 27.

55. No traces remain of this Roman hermitage and we do not even know exactly where it was located. W. Franke places it among the mountains of Subiaco, near the famous abbey. (W. Franke, *Romuald von Camaldoli und seine Reformtatigkeit zur Zeit Ottos III*, Berlin Historischen Studien 107, 1913, p.218.)

56. V5F, pp.38–39.

57. V5F, p.98.

58. V5F, p.41.

59. M. Cordovani, *Itinerario della rinascita spirituale,* Roma, A.Belardetti, 1946, p.292.

60. VR, Chapter 28.

61. VR, Chapter 27.

62. Cf. V5F, p.77. Veneration of the holy hermit martyrs flourished at once among the local population. A church was built over their grave (VR, Chapter 28) and they were inscribed in the Canons of Martyrs. The Camaldolese Order celebrates their liturgical memorial on November 13th. In Poland they are numbered among the country's patron saints.

63. This is the *Life of the Five Brothers,* already quoted many times, written by St. Bruno Boniface of Querfurt around 1005. This is a document of primary importance for the history of Romuald and especially the carrying out of his monastic reform!

64. VR, Chapter 27. St. Peter Damian writes of St. Bruno Boniface, his mission, and his martyrdom.

65. The 'proof of fire' or 'judgment of God' was a quasi–judicial procedure, mixed with religious convictions, used in the High Middle Ages. A decisive significance in discerning the truth was attached to the procedure, presuming an extraordinary intervention on the part of God by way of protection, or else condemnation.

66. VR, Chapter 27.

67. V5F, Introduction, p.21.

68. The Camaldolese liturgy celebrates the Feast of St. Bruno Boniface on February 12.

69. VR, Chapter 35.

70. VR, Chapter 37.

71. This is the monastery of St. Michael of Lemmo, in the Diocese of Parenzo. We will mention reclusion further on in this book.

72. VR, Chapter 31.

73. VR, Chapter 32. Monks from the Abbey of St. Benedict in the Alps near Muraglione Pass in the Forli area.

74. VR, Chapter 33. We presume that the saint kept his promise, but this has not come down to us in written form.

75. VR, Chapter 35.

76. Ibid.

77. Cf. A. Pagnani, *Vita di S. Romualdo abbate fondatore dei Camaldolesi,* Edizioni Camaldoli 1967, p.217.

78. Simony, along with concubinage, was one of the more painful and frequent wounds in the Church during the tenth and eleventh centuries. Various saints made it the reason for their healing work, *e.g.* St. Romuald, St. Peter Damian, St. John Gualbert, Pope St. Gregory VII.

79. VR, Chapter 35.

80. Ibid.

81. Ibid.

82. VR, Chapter 37. This is most probably the monastery of St. Mary in Silva, perhaps near Titignano between Orvieto and Terni, later suppressed by Pope Boniface VIII in 1297.

83. This is Bl. Guido or Guidino, still venerated in the Orvieto diocese.

84. VR, Chapter 37.

85. VR, Chapter 39.

86. VR, Chapter 42.

87. VR, Chapter 43.

88. VR, Chapter 46.

89. Sitria is a narrow valley stretching almost to the foot of Catria, about six kilometers from Fonte Avellana in the diocese of Nocera Umbra. The church, crypt, and some portions of a small monastery remain of St. Romuald's foundation. We can find no trace of the hermitage.

90. VR, Chapter 49.

91. St. Benedict, *Rule for Monasteries,* Ch.23, 25.

92. VR, Chapter 50.

93. Ibid.

94. VR, Chapter 49.

95. VR, Chapter 50. We do not know what this commentary touched upon. It is likely that Peter Damian had it in hand, in order to substantiate his observation about the poor grammatical style. Regarding the so–called *Salterio di S. Romualdo,* preserved at Camaldoli, we refer to the notes of the recent study: M.E. Magheri Cataluccio – A.U. Fossa, *Biblioteca e cultura a Camaldoli dal medioevo all 'umanesimo,* Rome, 1979 (Studia Anselmiana, 75), pp.8,9,30,182,183.

96. VR, Chapter 49.

97. James 3.17–18.

98. VR, Chapter 51.

99. VR, Chapter 64.

100. VR, Chapter 52.

101. Otto III died in 1002 and was succeeded by his cousin Henry II, Duke of Saxony, who was crowned at Rome in 1004.

102. This is the Abbey of Holy Savior. The actual city grew up around the abbey of the same name, founded by the Lombard king, Ratchis, in the 8th cent. Henry II gave it to Romuald in 1022.

103. VR, Chapter 65.

104. Ibid.

105. VR, Chapter 67.

106. VR, Chapter 69.

107. Ibid.

108. VR, Chapter 72.

109. Francisco Petrarcha, *Di Vita Solitaria,* Bk.II, Ch.16. in the Italian version by V. Bartoccetti, in: *Camaldolesi. Le figure piu espressive dell' Ordine,* Camaldoli, 1944, p.17.

110. VR, Chapter 69.

111. VR, Chapter 72.

112. R. Bartoletti, *S. Romualdo Ricognizione sepolcro,* Fabriano, 1981.

113. VR, Chapter 35.

114. VR, Chapter 39.

115. VR, Chapters 6, 8.

116. VR, Chapter 27.

117. VR, Chapter 10.

118. VR, Chapter 40.

119. VR, Chapter 13.

120. VR, Chapter 21.

121. VR, Chapter 9.

122. VR, Chapters 36, 43.

123. VR, Chapter 53.

124. VR, Chapter 17.

125. VR, Chapter 13.

126. VR, Chapter 53.

127. VR, Chapter 54.

128. VR, Chapter 55.

129. VR, Chapter 36.

130. VR, Chapter 59.

131. VR, Chapter 65.

132. VR, Chapter 50.

133. VR, Chapters 16, 31.

134. Cf. St. Augustine, *Commentary on the Psalms,* Ps. 32.

135. VR, Chapter 34.

136. VR, Chapter 40.

137. V5F, pp.33–34.

138. G. Cassiano, *Conferenze spirituali,* v.3, Edizioni Paoline, 1966.

139. V5F, pp.30–37.

140. Franke, *Romuald von Camaldoli.*

141. H.G. Voigt, *Brun von Querfurt,* Stuttgart, 1907.

142. The abbey of Grottaferrata, 22 km. from Rome, was founded by Abbot St. Nilus for a community of Greek Basilian monks who still live the monastic life there today.

143. For fuller notes, Cf. M. Della Santa, *Ricerche sull' idea monastica di S. Pier Damiano,* Edizioni Camaldoli, 1961 (studi e testi camaldolesi, 11), pp.194–195.

144. VR, Chapter 18.

145. VR, Chapter 22.

146. A. Giabbani, *L'eremo, Vita e spiritualita eremitica nel monachesimo camaldolese primitivo,* Brescia, Morcelliana, 1945, p.184.

147. Congregazione Camaldolese dell'Ordine di S. Benedetto. Regola di San Benedetto, Costituzioni e dichiarazioni, Camaldoli, 1985, p.119.

148. B. Rodolfo. *Regole della vita eremitica,* a cura di B. Ignesti, Subiaco, 1944 , pp.59,63. For a greater knowledge of the historical development of reclusion in the Camaldolese Order, we refer to G. Cacciamani: *La reclusione presso l'Ordine Camaldolese,* Edizioni Camaldoli, 1960.

149. Giabbani, *L'eremo,* p.185.

150. Cf. p.18.

151. V5F, p.41.

152. Cf. p.18.

153. M. Cordovani, 'Prefazione' a: P. Ciampelli. *Vita di S. Romualdo abate fondatore dei Camaldolesi,* Ravenna, 1927, p.6.

154. J. Leclercq. *S. Pier Damiano eremita e uomo di chiesa,* Brescia: Morcelliana, 1972, pp.23,25.

155. 'Dominus plane Martinus, qui in Camaldulensi eremo commoratur, vir videlicet diversis virtutibus adornatus... mihi retulit quod narro.' The letter is addressed, without specifying the name: 'Sir B. dearest brother, Peter Sinner–Monk greets you with fraternal love...' Migne, PL144,403.

156. VR, Chapter 69.

157. The hagiographical data about Bl. Rudolph are scarce. We already find him elected Prior of Camaldoli in 1074, succeeding Bl. Peter Dagnino, disciple of St. Romuald. He is the author of the *Rules for the Eremitical Life* in 2 drafts: the 1080 draft and a shorter version dated 1085. This is the oldest and most precious document in the eremitical tradition of the Hermitage at Camaldoli. To B. Rudolph is credited the transformation of the Hospice of Fonte Bono into the Monastery. Later he founded the Monastery of St. Peter in Luco di Mugello (FI) for nuns.

158. B. Rudolfo, *Regole,* pp.57–59.

159. Among the monasteries not founded by St. Romuald but which had already adopted the reform directives and had voluntarily requested annexation to Camaldoli, we mention: St. Justus and Clement of Volterra, St. Appollinare–in–Classe of Ravenna, St. Sepolcro, and others. Their absorption, further voluntary annexations and new foundations were to continue for about 3 centuries.

160. Before this year, 1113, they were simply known as Benedictines, sometimes called Romualdians or Hermits of Abbot Romuald (Cf. Pagnani, *Vita di S. Romualdo*, pp.337-338).

161. J. Mabillon, *Annales Ordinis S. Benedicti*, IV, 261.

162. G. Grandi, *Dissertationes Camaldulenses*, II, Lucca, 1707, pp.64–75.

163. G. Tabacco, 'La data di fondazione di Camaldoli,' in *Vita Monastica* XVI, 1962, 147–153.

164. Cf. Tabacco, p.149.

165. Cf. Pagnani, *Vita di S. Romualdo*, p.340.

166. Cf. pp. 49–50.

167. B. Rodolfo, *Regole*, p.15.

168. Tabacco, p.150.

169. Pagnani, *Vita di S. Romualdo*, pp.383–384.

170. AA.CC., III, App. coll. 243–245.

171. B. Rodolfo, *Regole*, pp.50–51, 54–55.

172. AA.CC., IV, p.103.

173. Cf. AA.VV., *Camaldolesi. Le figure piu espressive dell'Ordine*, Camaldoli, 1944, p.69.

174. G. Grandi, *Dissertationes Camaldulenses*, I, p.63.

175. Cf. I Cor. 12.4–6.

176. VR, Chapter 40.

177. Prb. 8.5.

178. VR, Chapters 5, 6.

179. VR, Chapter 27.

180. VR, Chapter 28.

181. Cf. p. 50.

182. *Camaldolesi*, p.40.

183. Cf. *Camaldolesi*, p.43.

184. Cf. A. Pagnani, *Storia dei Benedettini Camaldolesi*, Sassoferrato, 1949, p.41.

185. Cf. Mabillon, *Annales*, IV, 115; P. Ciampelli, *Guido Monaco* in 'Rivista Camaldolese,' II (1927), p.383.

186. St. Benedict, *Rule for Monasteries*, Prologue.

187. VR, Chapter 33.

188. P. Venturini, *Pier Damiani* in 'L'Avvenire,' Feb. 24, 1943. The text is referred to in *Camaldolesi*, p.58.

189. Ibid. p.59.

190. Pier Damiano, *Opera omnia*, III, Paris, 1743, p.396. The text is translated in *Camaldolesi*, p.59.

191. *Camaldolesi*, p.51.

192. Pier Damiano, *Carmina et preces*, carm. 213: Pl. 145, 968. M. Lokrantz, *L'opera poetica di S. Pier Damiani*, Stockholm, Almquist & Wiksell, 1964 p.72.

193. Cf. St. Benedict, *Rule for Monasteries*, Ch.2.

194. B. Rodolfo, *Regole*, p.15.

195. B. Rodolfo, *Regole*, pp.42–43, 60.

196. AA.CC., III, p.340.

197. Cf. AA.CC., III, pp.322–325.

198. G. Bonolis, 'Graziano' in *Enciclopedia Italiana* XVII, 781a.

199. Cf. *Camaldolesi*, p.89.

200. Cf. *Camaldolesi*, p.91.

201. The practice of changing one's name as a means for stressing a monk's distancing himself from the world, had already taken root in the monasteries for about half a century. For several years now, some have returned to the primitive custom which kept the baptismal name unchanged.

202. AA.CC., VIII, pp.341-342.

203. Zanobi Tantini, *Leggende di alcuni santi e beati venerati in S. Maria degli Angeli di Firenze,* Bologna, Romagnoli, 1864.

204. G. Vasari, *Le vite de' piu eccellenti pittori scultori ed architettori,* II, Florence, Sansoni, 1878, pp.17–26.

205. Cf. *Camaldolesi*, p.109.

206. B. Magni, *Storia dell'arte,* I, Rome, 1901, p.38.

207. Cf. *Camaldolesi*, p.109.

208. I Ricci, 'Bartolomeo Della Gatta' in *Rivista Camaldolese,* II, (1927), 272–274. See also Vasari, III, pp. 213–225.

209. Mt. 20. 26–27.

210. The first Italian translation of the *Hodoeporicon* by Vittorio Tamburnini is now in print, contributing to the centenary celebration of Traversari's birth (1386/1986): Ambrogio Traversari, *Hodoeporicon*, F. Le Monnier, Florence, 1985. Presentazione di Eugenio Garin.

211. Cf. A. Traversari, *Epistolarum*, XXIII, ep. 1, edited by L. Mehus, Florence, 1759, col. 955.

212. A nearly complete bibliography on Traversari up to 1985 can be found in the monograph: C. Somigli – T. Bargellini, *Ambrogio Traversari monaco camaldolese; la figura e la dottrina monastica*, Bologna, Edizioni Dehoniane / Edizioni Camaldoli, 1986, pp. 13–18.

213. The publication of the Acts of the International Conference held Sept. 16–18, 1986, at the monastery of Camaldoli and at the Central Office of Palazzo Strozzi, is now imminent. The Community of Camaldoli dedicated an entire issue of *Vita Monastica* (45: 1987), the quarterly on culture and monastic formation published by the monks, under the title 'Ambrogio Traversari camaldolese nel VI centenario dalla nascita 1386–1986.' The volume collects the contributions of various authors, an unpublished biography of Traversari, and the translation of book XV of his collected letters. The Acts of the Conference of Portico di Romagna are being printed at Traversari's native city.

214. Pagnani, *Storia*, p.164.

215. A very beautiful reproduction of Fra. Mauro's world map preserved at the St. Mark's Library in Venice was published by Tullia Gasparrini Leporace on the occasion of the seventh centenary of Marco Polo's birth, 1254/1954.

216. Cf. AA.CC., VII, pp.252–256.

217. Jerome Tiraboschi's text is taken from vol. 6 of *Storia della letteratura italiana,* quoted by Pagnani in *Storia*, p.170.

218. Cf. AA.CC., VII, pp.286–288.

219. *Camaldolesi,* p.161.

220. These notes are limited to the hagiographical dates and some mention of the more significant aspects of Gregory XVI's pontificate. For ampler and more documented information, see: AA.VV., *Gregorio XVI Miscellanea Commemorative,* 2v., published by the Camaldolese of St. Gregory al Celio, Rome, 1948.

221. Don Placid Zurla (Hyacinth Francis in baptism) was born at Legnago on April 2, 1769. He was a distinguished naturalist and theologian, a sought-after spiritual father who skillfully cultivated his love for liturgy and sacred chant. He was abbot of his monastery during the Napoleonic suppression. Invited by the abbot of St. Gregory al Celio, Don Maur Cappellari, he transferred to Rome and devoted himself to teaching. Pope Pius VII made him a cardinal on March 10, 1823, and Pope Leo XII named him Vicar of the Rome diocese on Jan. 3, 1824. He died in Palermo, Oct. 29, 1834.

222. Papal infallibility was defined as dogmatic truth in the Constitution *'Pastor aeturnus,'* of the Vatican Council I, July 18, 1870.

223. The monastery of St. Gregory al Celio *ad Clivum Scauri* was founded by St. Gregory the Great in 575 on the site of his familial home on the Celian Hill. He dedicated it to St. Andrew the Apostle, introduced the Rule of St. Benedict and became its abbot. When Gregory was Pope, the monastery's prior, St. Augustine of Canterbury, departed to evangelize the Anglo–Saxons of England. In 1573, the Camaldolese took the place of the Benedictines there.

224. See note 220.

225. VR, Chapter 35.

226. Pagnani, *Vita di S. Romualdo*, p.320.

227. VR, Chapter 63.

228. 'A certain wondrous monk called Romuald who renewed the practices of ancient equity among the sexes, and on an equal footing for both...' *Liber tramitis aevi Odilonis abbatis,* ed. P. Dinter, Siegburg, 1980, p.3.

229. Cf. pp.65–67.

230. This is what the Camaldolese chroniclers state: 'It existed near the river Arno, at a place called Rosano, under the patronage of Saint Mary, about which we will have later information; for it became part of another of our monasteries in the twelfth century, St. John the Evangelist of Pratovecchio.' (AA.CC., II, pp.147-148). Cf. Pagnani, *Storia*, pp.61, 63.

231. Pagnani, *Storia*, p.61.

232. Cf. pp.81-87.

233. Pagnani, *Storia*, p.62.

234. CJC, canon 615.

235. Cf. pp.96–97.

236. Cf. p.104.

237. Cf. pp.105–110.

238. V. Meneghin, *S. Michele in Isola di Venezia*, I, Venezia, 1962. See pp. 461–471 regarding the suppression of the monastery and the monks' attempts to recover.

239. Vasari, *Le Storie*, II, p.18. Dante Alighieri remembers him in the *Purgatorio*, Canto 26.

240. Pagnani, *Storia*, pp.70–71.

241. See pp.87–88.

242. D. Savelli, *Il convento di S. Maria degli Angeli a Firenze*, Florence, Tornatre, 1983, p.8.

243. Vasari, III, pp.213–225.

244. Vasari, II, pp.24–25.

245. See pp.81–85.

246. See pp.90–96.

247. Cf. G. Cioci, *Cenni storici del Sacro Eremo di Camaldoli*, Florence, 1864, p.241.

248. Andrea di Strumi, *Vita di S. Giovanni Gualberto*, in G. Spinelli — G. Rossi, *Alle origini di Vallombrosa*, Milano, Jaca Book 1984, p.71.

249. AA.CC.,IV, pp.192–193. The desired spot was Cerreta where there is now a forestry nursery about one kilometer south of monastery.

250. AA.CC.,V, p.132.

251. Martino III, *Vetus Ordo divinorum officiorum,* AA.CC.,VI, App., coll. 66–203.

252. Martino III, *Constitutiones Camaldulenses Ordinis 'De Moribus' in tres libros partitae,* AA.CC., VI, App., coll. 1–65.

253. AA.CC., V, p.195. B. Ignesti, *I beati Peregrine e Simone eremiti del S. Eremo di Camaldoli,* in 'Rivista Camaldolese,' II (1927): 536–543.

254. The problems of a *collegio* or better, school for boys in Fontebono—as the Monastery of Camaldoli came to be called until the 16th cent. —were already present in the 15th cent: Cf. Magheri Cataluccio–Fossa, *Biblioteca e cultura,* pp.100–116. But formation's worry was not unrelated to what Ruldolph faced in the 11th cent., though in this case, regarding adult aspirants to the eremitical life. Cf. B. Rodolfo, *Regole,* p.61. See also: Magheri Cataluccio – Fossa, pp.20–21.

255. AA.CC.,VI, p.322.

256. A. Traversari, *Epistole* lib. XV, ep. 21, ed. Mehus, col. 691. This letter like all of book XV of the collection of Traversari's letters has been translated by Somigli: Cf. C. Somigli, *Le Lettere di Ambrogio Traversari a Mariotto Allegri (1423–1439)* in 'Vita Monastica,' n.45, Camaldoli, 1987, pp.154–236.

257. This capitular decision has justly been determined the 'Magna Carta' of the Camaldolese Order regarding studies. Cf. Magheri Cataluccio—Fossa, *Biblioteca e cultura,* pp.103–104.

258. Peter Delfino, a monk of St. Michael of Murano, was Prior General for 45 years. He was the last Prior General 'for life,' a man of renowned culture and learning. During his governing of the Congregation its unity was seriously corroded by a break–off group of hermits. His role as superior still needs to be investigated for the most part, but it is often discussed. It is commonly held that he was a man and monk of holy life. Peter died at St. Michael on Jan. 15, 1525.

259. Cf. AA.CC.,VII, pp.365–366. See also: G. Cacciamani, *Camaldoli cittadella di Dio,* Edizione Paoline, Roma, 1968, pp.33-36.

260. Vasari. *Le vite,* I, p.683.

261. 'Guido, guardian of the Camaldolese hospital *(Guido custos hospitalis Camaldulensis)'* AA.CC., II, p. 109. See also: P. Ciampelli, *Guida storica illustrata di Camaldoli e S. Eremo,* Bagno di Romagna, 1926, pp.51–52.

262. Cf. Ciampelli, *Guida,* pp. 52–53.

263. AA.CC., VIII, pp.131–134.

264. C. Pierucci, *Fonte Avellana: mille anni di storia,* in 'Il papa a Fonte Avellana,' Camaldoli, 1983 ('Vita Monastica' 33), p.32.

265. Pierucci, p.44.

266. See pp.23, 24, 27, 29.

267. A rich collection of testimony for and against the fact of Dante's stay at Fonte Avellana can be found in C. Somigli's *L'ombra di Dante a Fonte Avellana,* Fonte Avellana, 1984.

268. These are Don Anselm Giabbani, Don Bernard Ignesti and Don Ramiro Merloni.

269. Text taken from 'L'omelia di sua santita Giovanni Paolo II alla Messa celebrata nel Monastero di Fonte Avellana,' in 'Il papa a Fonte Avellana,' pp. 7,9,11.

270. From 'Il saluto del papa alla Communita dei Monaci,' in 'Il papa a Fonte Avellana,' p.13.

271. From the very first documentation and during successive centuries, 'Fonte Bono' or 'Fonte Bona' always refers to the Monastery, while 'Camaldoli' usually refers to the Hermitage.

272. St. Benedict, *Rule for Monasteries,* ch. 53.

273. B. Rodolfo, *Le regole,* p.34.

274. B. Rodolfo, p.35.

275. See p.173, note 4.

276. Gerado, *Constitutiones Camaldulenses a. 1279 seu Liber IV de Moribus,* AA.CC., VI. App., col. 240–255.

277. AA.CC., II, p.109.

278. Cf. *Camaldolesi,* pp.211–214.

279. AA.CC., VI. App., col. 62.

280. AA.CC., VI. App., col. 10.

281. Cf. L. Bartolini, *Attivita beneficia di Camaldoli,* in 'Rivista Camaldolese,' I (1926): 132–136.

282. Cf. G. Bacchi, *Camaldoli di Firenze,* in 'Rivista Camaldolese,' I (1926):164–168, and *S. Benedetto fuori della Porta a Pinti di Firenze,* in 'Rivista Camaldolese,' II (1927): 449–456.

283. Peter Damian, *Opusculi* IX, PL. 145, 212a.

284. G. Cacciamani, *L'antica foresta di Camaldoli; storia e codice forestale,* Edizioni Camaldoli, 1965.

285. The Camaldolese Constitutions of 1629, quoted by G. Cioci, *Cenni storici del Sacro Eremo di Camaldoli,* Florence, 1864, pp.90–91.

286. From the same Constitutions of 1629, quoted by Cacciamani, p.11.

287. E. Repetti, *Dizionario geografico fisico storico della Toscana,* I, Florence, 1833, p.403.

288. For the composition of this particular chapter we are indebted to: A Pagnani, *Storia,* pp.125–129, and also *Camaldolesi,* pp.146–153.

289. AA.CC., VII. App., col. 293–328.

290. Cf. P. Giustiniani—P. Quirini, *Libellus ad Leonem X*, AA.CC., IX App., col. 683. See also: S. Tramontin, *Un Programma di riforma della chiesa per il concilio Lateranese V: il 'Libellus ad Leonem X' dei veneziani Paolo Giustiniani e Pietro Quirini*, in 'Venezia e i concili,' Quaderini del Laurentianum, Venezia, 1962, pp.76–78.

291. Cordovani, *Itinerario*, p.292.

292. Dante Alighieri, *Paradisio*, XXI, 115.

293. St. Benedict, *Rule for Monasteries*, ch. 58.

294. Cf. Is. 40.3; Mt. 3.3.

295. Vatican Council II., Decr. *'Perfectae caritatis,'* 25.

296. *Vita Monastica,* quarterly of spirituality, history and monastic issues... Direction and Administration, 52010 Camaldoli (Arezzo), Florence 11031523, Edizioni Camaldoli. *Lettere agli amici,* periodical compilation. Camaldoli (AR).

297. *Campo Amabile, Fonte Bono:* the first and most ancient names for the Hermitage and Monastery of Camaldoli, respectively.

298. A very ancient tradition traced to the beginnings and codified by Prior B. Rudolf IV of Camaldoli in his *Constitutiones* of 1085, has preferred the title of 'Prior' or 'Prior General' to 'Abbot' which is normative for the Benedictine tradition. The historical traditions seem to be traceable to the fact that at the time of the Congregation of Camaldoli's formation, the figure of 'abbot' as outlined in St. Benedict's *Rule* was considered almost everywhere as somewhat decadent vis-a-vis its primitive role as 'father of souls,' becoming more a 'guardian of law' or 'leader.' We suppose a reaction at the root of this preference, tending to maintain the abbatial 'service' but discarding the suspect title. However, this tradition remained unchanged and limited only by the formation of Camaldoli itself. The name indicated in the *Rule* was peacefully applied elsewhere.

299. St. Peter Damian, *Opusculum* XI, 5–6.

Glossary

Abbot / Abbey Abbot is the title given to the superior of a monastery called an Abbey. Abbots are found among the monastic Orders and some Orders of Canons. Abbatial insignia are comparable to those of the episcopacy: ring, mitre, crozier. The founders of Camaldoli itself decided not to raise it to the abbatial status, though many of the other historical Camaldolese foundations were abbeys.

Apostolic See Designating the official seat/throne of a bishop, the See is Apostolic when it refers to the See of Rome, associated with Apostles Peter and Paul. 'Apostolic See' is often used in a context of power or jurisdiction.

Avellanita The Avellanita Congregation developed around the 'Venerable Hermitage' of Fonte Avellana which dates back to c. 1000 AD. This Congregation, growing parallel to the Camaldolese Congregation, was joined to the Camaldolese family in 1570.

Benedictines What came to be known as the Benedictine Order developed gradually during the centuries following the death of St. Benedict of Nursia (mid–6th century). As one among many monastic rules, the *Rule of St. Benedict* gradually gained precedence and was set as the Empire's standard by St. Benedict of Aniane in 817. Benedictine abbeys are autonomous, but exist within congregations which form the Benedictine Confederation.

Bull, Papal The Papal *Bulla* (seal) marks a written command of the Pope. During the nineteenth century, only the most important Bulls have been actually sealed this way in wax.

Camaldoli / Camaldolese Camaldoli is the motherhouse of the Camaldolese Congregation. Situated near Arezzo in Tuscany, Camaldoli comprises both a hermitage and a monastery. The Prior General normally resides at Camaldoli.

Canon Throughout the centuries of Church history, 'Canon' has been used chiefly to refer to: the official list of inspired books of Scripture; liturgical rules and the consecratory prayer of the Eucharist; juridical norms; ecclesiastical disciplinary decisions; secular clergy belonging to a cathedral; a member of the semi–monastic Order following the *Rule of St. Augustine* (post 10th c.).

Cell The monastic 'cell' refers to the room or set of rooms used by the monk or nun particularly so among the eremitical expressions of the religious life.

Cenobite / Cenobium A Cenobite (from the Greek words for 'common' and 'life') is a member of a monastic Order living in community. The Cenobium is a monastery composed of monks / nuns, living communally rather than as hermits. The Camaldolese Congregation comprises both of these characteristic monastic modes of life.

Chapter / Capitular Originally referring to a section of a monastic Rule, and the gathering of monks / nuns to listen to the reading of that Rule or some spiritual instruction, Chapter also came to refer to the gathering of community members or representatives for decision–making purposes. The members of the monastery who enjoy full membership juridically are members of the Chapter, or capitulars. The gathering–place for Chapter became known as the Chapter 'room' or 'house.'

Cloister The cloister is that part of a monastery or convent which is enclosed and 'off–limits,' wherein the religious reside and to which access from the outside is restricted.

Commendam Abbot A person, whether lay, clerical or religious, who has been granted an ecclesiastical benefice of 'abbot,' thereby enjoying the revenues of such an office without actually fulfilling its role. This custom generally led to abuse, and not surprisingly, often to degeneration of monastic observance.

Concubinage The act of living together as husband and wife outside the formal married state.

Congregation A group of monastic houses—often originally formed along national, ethnic or linguistic lines—united at first for the purposes of discipline and reform, and later for centralization. The current official name of the Camaldolese Congregation is: *The Camaldolese Congregation of the Order of Saint Benedict.*

Conversatio *Conversatio morum* is one of the traditional Benedictine monastic vows, along with obedience and stability, as well as the other evangelical counsels of poverty and chastity. Conversatio pertains to the faithfulness one brings to living the monastic manner of life, conditioned by the history and traditions of a particular monastic interpretation of that life.

Conversi A term used to refer to the institution of monastic 'lay brothers' which arose during medieval times. A *conversus* did not take solemn vows as such, was not bound to the normal choir duty, and did not possess 'Chapter' rights.

Doge The doge (variant of *duce,* leader) of Venice was the chief magistrate for the Venetian republic. The first doge was Saint Lawrence Giustiniani, 1381–1455.

Don Corresponding to the French title 'Dom,' Don will be used to signify a professed member of a monastic Order, but also as a title for any distinguished man.

Eremo / Eremiticism Derived from the Greek word for desert, *eremo* signifies hermitage. Eremiticism, or hermit life, has been present in both the Eastern and Western Churches in one form or another during most of the Church's history down to present times.

General Chapter The regular canonical/juridical assembly held by a religious Congregation or Order for the purposes of holding elections, enacting legislation, reviewing visitations and monitoring various aspects of religious life. An 'extraordinary' General Chapter is one convened outside the normal rotation for some specific purpose.

Habit The distinctive garb worn by the religious. The Camaldolese white habit now consists of a tunic, cincture, scapular and hood. The cowl is worn for choir and the mantle is worn by some monks outdoors.

Hermeneutical Signifies an interpretative approach toward a given phenomenon.

Hermit / Hermitage Generally, a hermit is one who lives a solitary manner of life for religious purposes, accenting solitude, mindfulness and contemplation. Hermits exist officially within the Western Church in an organized way, e.g. Camaldolese Congregation O.S.B.; Camaldolese Hermits of Monte Corona; Carthusian Order. See *Eremo/Eremiticism* above.

Mendicant The Mendicant or 'begging' Orders were originally the Franciscan and Dominican Friars, though the term was later extended to the Servites, Carmelites and Augustinian Hermits. They did not own property and did not bind themselves by the monastic vow of stability. Mission appeals are contemporary examples of 'mendicant' activity among the friars.

Monk / Monastery A religious who has bound himself by vows (stability, obedience, *conversatio morum*, chastity, poverty) to a monastic manner of life within the context of a community living a monastic rule. The monastery is the residence for a monastic community.

Nicolaitism (Nicolaitanism) refers to clerics who do not remain celibate, but either marry or have sexual relationships with concubines.

Novice / Novitiate The novice is the religious member during the beginning probationary period of religious life. Normally the novice enters this novitiate time after an initial period of postulancy.

Nun A religious woman living under solemn vows within a cloister.

Obedience Not only refers to the moral virtue and evangelical counsel of obedience, but also to an assignment or command given to a religious by a superior.

Oblate Originally referring to a child dedicated to a monastery by parents, 'oblate' came to signify a lay person living with the monastic community or in some other close connection with it.

Oratory Literally a place of prayer (Latin: *oratorium*), oratory usually refers to the area where a monastic community celebrates the liturgical hours, *i.e.* Divine Office, *Opus Dei.*

Pilgrimage The devotional practice of travelling to holy places *(e.g.* tombs, shrines, churches), very popular during medieval times.

Postulant / Postulancy (Aspirant, candidate) one experiencing that initial stage within religious life prior to novitiate. This period of postulancy can last months or years, depending on the local custom and/ or Constitutions of the religious group.

Prior / Priory Within the Benedictine tradition, the term 'prior' has usually referred to the monk next in rank to the abbot, who substituted for the abbot in his absence. Camaldoli developed a tradition of having priors instead of abbots. Today the Camaldolese Benedictines have only priors as superiors. The priory is the house/community presided over by a prior.

Procurator Ultimately the monastic business manager or overseer, often fulfilling the roles of accountant, business manager and guardian of stock and provisions. Another historical role for a 'procurator' has been serving as a liaison for the general membership with various temporal and ecclesiastical powers.

Profession The act of committing oneself through vows or promises to God's service in the context of a religious community, after fulfilling the initial formational requirements of postulancy and novitiate. The profession can be simple (temporary) or solemn (definitive, lifelong).

Recluse / Reclusion A recluse is a hermit who lives in a state of greater solitude and enclosure. Reclusion, which is canonically found only within the Camaldolese congregations, can be semi–reclusion, temporary reclusion, or permanent reclusion.

Regula The Latin word for Rule. Within the Camaldolese Benedictine context, this term usually refers to the *Rule of St. Benedict,* but sometimes also to the various 'regulae' for hermits composed by various Romualdian/ Camaldolese monks/hermits.

Romualdian The Romualdian movement developed around the person, example and vision of St. Romuald of Ravenna (c.950–1027), particularly during the tenth, eleventh and twelfth centuries.

Sarcophagus A stone coffin used by Christians and non–Christians for burial. Sarcophagi were often decorated in relief chiselled onto the exterior.

Schism A formal separation from Church unity. Schismatics are not necessarily heretics, though they can be both.

Simony / Simoniacal   Simony refers to the purchase/sale of ecclesiastical offices, orders and benefices. Simoniacal transactions were notorious during the eleventh century and were vigorously opposed by Romualdians and other like–minded reformers.

Synod   A formal meeting, usually in the context of a local Church area, convened to address questions of ecclesiastical discipline or teaching.

Vicar   From the Latin *vicarius,* 'substitute,' vicar refers to one who stands in the status of 'second place' so as to perform the superior's duties when the latter is absent or incapacitated.

Vigils   A particularly monastic practice, keeping vigils can refer to the celebration of the liturgical hours of the Divine Office during the night, or to the ascetical practice of remaining awake and prayerful throughout the night.

Visitator / Visitation   Within the context of Camaldolese life this refers to the periodic, formal inspection of the spiritual and temporal welfare of a given community. This act is performed by the Visitators who are elected by the General Chapter.